Fonteyn the making of a legend

KEITH MONEY

Fonteyn

REYNAL & COMPANY
in association with
WILLIAM MORROW AND COMPANY, INC.

1974

the making of a legend

Published in the United States in 1974

Text copyright © 1973 by Keith Money

Photographs copyright © 1973 as indicated in photographers' credits

First published in Great Britain by William Collins Sons & Co. Ltd., 1973

Printed in Switzerland by Conzett + Huber, Zurich

Book designed by Keith Money

Library of Congress Catalog Card Number 74-3578

ISBN 0-688-61163-X

for B. Q.
for Madam
and
for Fred

Acknowledgments

I WOULD LIKE TO THANK Mrs. Hilda Hookham, and Mr. Felix Hookham, for sparing me much time and material concerning their daughter; Mr. Felix Fonteyn, for help with photographs of his sister; Mr. Koji Saito, for somehow managing to compile an exhaustive file of photo copies from countless sources – a collection which often set me on the trail of some picture or other, the existence of which I might not have suspected otherwise; Miss Mary Clarke of *The Dancing Times,* for giving generously of her time and her own well-organized filing system; Miss Neil Ambrose, for putting a brave and cheerful face on my pillaging countless items from her colossal series of Fonteyn scrapbooks; her industriousness has proved invaluable. Miss Patricia Stone, for allowing me total access to her remarkable diaries, as well as early prints; the Victoria and Albert Museum, for help with Mr. Gordon Anthony's negatives; Miss Pamela May, for unearthing a valuable programme and other memorabilia; also the Misses Good, and Miss Jennie Walton, for contributing important prints; Mr. Peter Williams of *Dance and Dancers,* for advice and practical help; also Mrs. Joan Stafford, and Miss Gillian Warren, both of whom spared time and energy. My particular thanks must go to Mrs. Joy Brown, for sustaining my courage at difficult moments, often by trans-Atlantic telephone. Individually I would wish to thank the very many photographers whose work appears in this book, and those critics whom I have re-quoted. Encouragement and interest from young people, particularly in America, has been a rewarding feature of this task.

Quintessentially, my thanks are due to Margot, most particularly for not resisting this book with even greater determination – doubtless within her compass, but something the book could *not* have survived. Like an old mariner, this editor knows he has been to sea, through diverse weathers and rocky straits. One or two mementos from distant lands have been swept overboard, but lo! the cargo is saved.

K. M.

Introduction

Some years have passed since I first found myself surrounded by a nucleus of material for an earlier book on Margot Fonteyn. Even as I put it together I was aware of its inadequacy as any real picture of her art. At best, it was only one arch, and it seemed there should be at least an attempt to record the entire arcade, in the belief that it would have validity both historically and as an inspiration to younger generations: an example of what can be accomplished by one body if the right sylphides attend the christening, and if the godchild strives thereafter to do them honour. It should also prove that a dedicated life does not necessarily preclude any other life.

For myself I must plead that this volume is a personal view of a public personality in that the choice of a picture has finally come to the one which has struck some particular chord with this editor's view of his subject, though there has always been the underlying intention to itemize the performing career as comprehensively as possible.

Though surprisingly few of Fonteyn's adult rôles appear to have escaped the photographer's net, there are some omissions: I could find nothing of her in the original costume for Lilian in "The Lord of Burleigh" (not surprisingly, since the ballet was well established in the company's repertoire by the time the young Fonteyn was given a chance in the sisters' pas de deux, with Markova) and last-minute appearances in "Prometheus," "Cupid and Psyche" and "Promenade" went unrecorded, as did her initial venture into "Carnaval" (as Papillon). A photograph does exist of "Checkmate," taken in Paris, where a line-up of Pawns included Fonteyn, but I have not wasted space with it, since there seems little point in naming a row of identical little figures in a rather murky stage shot. On the other hand, her partners should all be found here, somewhere, completing a roll-call of well over thirty.

Wherever possible I have tried to use photographs that have not been published before, and though some, of necessity, may appear familiar, a high proportion are in fact making their début on the printed page. The pictorial index of rôles at the end of the book provides a further choice. It has not been easy to select from such a mass of material, and the discards from even the short-list mounted steadily, but I believe those that are left give a comprehensive view. For the interested wanderer, I hope this book will prove a guidepath to an astonishing life – the individual vistas perhaps flashing past too quickly, but all the milestones clearly marked.

K. M.

She was born on 18th May 1919, in a house called North Red-lands beside the railway station of Reigate in Surrey. The second child of Felix and Hilda Hookham, she was christened Margaret Evelyn but soon became known as Peggy, to avoid confusion with an aunt and great-aunt both named Margaret. Her parents are both English, though Mrs. Hookham's family is half Brazilian. Peggy's elder brother Felix soon became the idol of her young life. By the time she was two, the family had moved nearer London, to the outlying suburb of Ealing; to 44 Waldeck Road.

The path to a career in dancing began for Margot Fonteyn as it has for so many a young girl: with the local dancing class. In this particular instance, a casual remark by Mr. Hookham on the possibility of deportment classes being needed for his daughter was taken seriously by Mrs. Hookham. Deportment classes as such being unavailable in the district, she proceeded to explore the suitability of the local dancing class, which advertised on the brass plate of a nearby gate in Ealing. Peggy, on whose behalf this exploration took place, was at this time a composed and silent child not given greatly to utterances of any kind. But perhaps because of this fact, once enrolled at the classes, she

*Miss Bosustow's
class, Ealing*

FELIX HOOKHAM

On the road, in Louisville, Kentucky. Right, homework

FELIX HOOKHAM

created an impression of sweetness and originality. Indeed, according to her new teacher Miss Grace Bosustow, Peggy was possessed of the most perfect grace.

She was soon chosen to lead eight fellow pupils onto the stage, in a number called *The Little Co-Optimists;* Peggy deemed by Miss Bosustow to be absolutely reliable for the task. It was already apparent that Peggy, despite her quiet and rather uncommunicative manner, was clearly determined to excel in the company of other children. Without in any way being tiresome about it, she appeared concerned to be 'best', a position which could only be attained (as she seemed to realise at an exceptionally early age) by application and work.

With her mother, on board ship

With her brother, at Ventnor

In the Middlesex County Times of July 5th 1924, came the first of countless enthusiastic reviews destined to follow: "In the 'Silver Ballet' there was a remarkably fine solo dance by Peggy Hookham, which was vigorously encored."

At a subsequent date we learn that "…Miss Peggy Hookham gave a spirited rendering of the tambourine dance", the instrument being used "with great vivacity".

During Peggy's first years at dancing class she was taken by her mother to a matinée at the Palace Theatre, where, from a side seat in the Upper Circle, she watched Madame Pavlova dance. Peggy was mainly interested to see that some of the steps she herself was learning were also demonstrated by the lady on stage; however the memory of the performance seems to have

faded quickly under the usual jumble of childhood stimuli.

At the age of eight she found her horizons widening dramatically: her father was posted abroad as Consultant Engineer to the British American Tobacco Company. Minus Felix, who remained at boarding school, the family crossed to the United States. There was some sporadic schooling for Peggy while Mr. Hookham completed his study of the tobacco growing methods of the southern states, preparatory to his main posting: the China Organization of the tobacco company, starting in Tientsin, later in Hong Kong, and then, more permanently, in Shanghai. From the family's base in China, periodically Mrs. Hookham and her daughter travelled back to England to visit Felix.

It was in London that Peggy was, for the first time, really fascinated by the sight of someone dancing on a stage: Alicia Markova, appearing as a guest artist with the embryonic Vic-Wells Ballet Company. Peggy's marked aversion to "difficult steps" and her pleasure in more simple "Greek-type" dancing, did not prevent her saying to her mother after Miss Markova's performance: "That's what I want to do."

With the young girl's first positive statement singling out dancing from amongst her other interests, Mrs. Hookham promptly arranged for several lessons with Nicholas Legat before they returned to China. The rôles taken by Miss Hookham at school performances in China were as numerous as they were varied. Some of them even echoed her earliest efforts for Miss Bosustow back in Ealing. It was noted in a local newspaper:

"Miss Peggy Hookham was easily the hit of the performance with her clever dancing, the little girl's footwork being especially striking in the dance of a Turkish slave-girl where she jangled her tambourine and flung herself into the dance with a gay abandon rare in such a [young] dancer."

Dancing class matinées soon become a regular feature of Peggy's life in Shanghai. There she appears as Pan (left) in the Romer-Peeler School's production of Pipes of Pan. In 1930 she also takes part in a Shanghai production of Hansel and Gretel

The first public picture of the future Margot Fonteyn appears in the September 1931 issue of The Dancing Times (below). Already, her name is subjected to alteration. The caption reads:

"Dragon Sprites

"Veronica Clifton and Peggi Hookham, pupils of the Romer-Peeler School in Shanghai as they appeared in the Concert given in April by the Royal Society of St. George, Shanghai"

A dancing teacher of the time is busy advertising on the following page: "Rumba Rhythm and Danzón (America's latest craze), also Parisian and Modified Argentine Tango, Society Lilt, etc."

In Shanghai, Mrs. Hookham was fortunate in discovering an imaginative teacher, George Gontcharov, formerly a pupil in St. Petersburg. He devised some private classes shared between Peggy, her friend June Bear (later Brae) and a young American friend of theirs. The classes took place in Mrs. Bear's tiny sitting room, with Mrs. Bear playing the piano after a fashion while Mr. Gontcharov gave the three girls their class. Speaking of Peggy, Gontcharov was to say later: "Directly I saw her I knew she had a *ballerina's* head. Her face – she was very attractive, with big dark eyes – seemed to talk to me. She held herself beautifully. She was always somehow *intent,* as though she had some idea that she knew what she was about."

17

For a growing girl, the costumes worn in Shanghai are regenerated in different guises…

In London again, in 1933, Mrs. Hookham and Peggy prepared for their next hurdle: would this girl, so far lacking any real comparative assessment, be considered sufficiently promising material by any teacher of renown? Mrs. Hookham singled out the Princess Seraphine Astafieva as the first target, for the Princess assumed the greatest importance as being the teacher of Alicia Markova, and it was the example of Markova that had set Peggy's thoughts firmly – and one might guess, irrevocably – on the path to becoming a ballet dancer of some sort. Mrs. Hookham finally gained an appointment with the Princess, who ex-

plained that she did not wish to receive any more pupils. Mrs. Hookham countered desperately with the startling information that she had come all the way from Shanghai just to bring her daughter to the Princess. Astafieva, it seems, remained impassively remote even when faced with this news, yet she did agree, finally to 'look'. With the 'look', there came a new degree of tolerance; it was decided that Peggy could attend classes. Astafieva felt that the young girl would also need private lessons every day, and that she should come to the bigger classes – but at an additional fee. However the classes were worth it, the Princess had the ability to remove the horror from the 'difficult' steps, and for Peggy there came an understanding of the meaning that might be invested in the merest technicality, so that it became, if not easy, then at least surmountable.

Six months were spent under Astafieva's tuition, until Mrs. Hookham became anxious that her daughter's capabilities should be assessed in a more definite way. She wished to take Peggy for an audition at the Vic-Wells Ballet run by Ninette de Valois in North London. There, they would be able to tell a mother whether her daughter was ready to go on the stage. Astafieva responded to this latest suggestion with a certain frostiness, but she conceded that perhaps Peggy should try for an audition.

It proved successful, and Miss Peggy Hookham entered, as a result, her first really theatrical environment: The Sadler's Wells Theatre in Rosebery Avenue, Finsbury; managed – like the Old Vic – by the already legendary Lilian Baylis. The environment was spartan if historic. It was at Sadler's Wells, during a morning class conducted by Ursula Moreton (who had approved Peggy at her audition) that Ninette de Valois entered and cast her far-seeing eyes over the assembly. A famous exchange followed:

"Who's the little Chinese-looking girl in the corner?" she enquired of Miss Moreton, who whispered in reply:

"She's not Chinese. Her name's Hookham."

"Well, where does she come from?" countered de Valois, curiosity unassuaged.

"She's from Shanghai," replied Miss Moreton, conceding the match.

"There – what did I tell you!" exclaimed de Valois as she departed, satisfied.

To claim de Valois' attention to such an extent was tanta-mount to passing a second audition.

It was soon after her arrival at Sadler's Wells that Peggy was numbed by the news of Astafieva's death. However, the die had been cast and she determined to do well in her new job, for the chance of a real career lay before her.

STUDIO IRIS

THE OLD VIC.

Founded by Emma Cons, December 26th, 1880

SADLER'S WELLS

(Re-opened January 6th, 1931)

Lessee and Manager of both Theatres:
LILIAN BAYLIS, C.H., M.A. Oxon. (Hon ,) LL.D. Birm. (Hon).
Hon. Co-Director with Lilian Baylis of Opera and Ballet - GEOFFREY TOYE

SEASON, 1934-5

The Vic-Wells Ballet

First Night of Ballet Season

AT SADLER'S WELLS:

Tuesday, October 2nd, 1934 at 8.30 p.m.

Choreographist and Ballet Mistress	..	..	Ninette de Valois
Assistant Ballet Mistress	..	.. ..	Ursula Moreton
Musical Director ..	.. ..	.. ..	Constant Lambert

OLD VIC., Waterloo Road, S.E.1	Box Office, Telephone—Hop 3424, 3426
SADLER'S WELLS, Rosebery Av., E.C.1	Box Office, Telephone—Clerkenwell 1121, 1122

PROGRAMME PRICE 3d.

The Haunted Ballroom

A Ballet in two scenes.
Written and composed by Geoffrey Toye.
Choreography by Ninette de Valois.
Costumes and Decor by Motley.

Scene I.—While a ball is in progress in another part of the house young Treginnis is persuaded by three of his father's guests to show them the haunted ballroom. They are enchanted with the room and express their desire to dance. The boy begs them not to do this, and tries to explain the terrors of the room. Suddenly the Master of Treginnis enters. He is furious with his son and orders him to bed. Left alone with his guests he tells them how all his ancestors met their death in this ballroom. He asks them to leave, and he realises he is doomed to the fate of his ancestors.

Scene II.—The same some hours later. A Stranger Player summons the ghostly dancers, and three of these resemble the young girls who had raided the room earlier. The Master of Treginnis enters. He sees the Stranger Player and asks him the identity of his companions. He is told they are dancers and that they will not dance unless he will lead them. He tears off his dressing gown and dances. They all join in. In his delirium he sees his three guests, and endeavours to dance with one of them—Alicia. The dance becomes wilder and terror seizes him as he realises they will not let him stop, and that he cannot escape. He eventually dances himself to death.

A ghostly bell awakens the house to the tragedy. They find him and carry him away, and young Treginnis is left with the growing realisation that the fate of his father awaits him one day.

CAST :

The Master of Treginnis	ROBERT HELPMANN
Young Treginnis	MARGOT FONTES
Alicia	ALICIA MARKOVA
Ursula	URSULA MORETON
Beatrice	BEATRICE APPLEYARD
The Stranger Player	WILLIAM CHAPPELL

Ghosts—
HERMIONE DARNBOROUGH, JOY NEWTON, SHEILA McCARTHY, WENDA HORSBURGH, PEGGY MELLISS, JOY ROBSON, JILL GREGORY, ELIZABETH MILLER, DORIS MAY, MOLLY BROWN, GWYNETH MATHEWS, NADINA NEWHOUSE
CLAUDE NEWMAN, WALTER GORE, ROLLO GAMBLE.

Butler	CAROL BERTRAM
Footmen	MAURICE BROOKE, LESLIE EDWARDS

Conducted by the Composer.

———— :: ————

———— : INTERVAL : ————

2nd October is the opening night of the new season at Sadler's Wells. Margot Fontes takes the mime rôle of the Young Treginnis in *The Haunted Ballroom*, by de Valois, as well as dancing in a new *pas de quatre* of *Les Rendezvous*. During the rehearsals for this revival she encounters, for the first time, the choreographer Frederick Ashton.

She also appears in the small rôle of Lilian in Ashton's *The Lord of Burleigh*, dancing a *pas de deux* with her great idol Markova.

20th November; Margot Fontes appears as a cygnet in *Le Lac des Cygnes* at a Charity Gala for Queen Charlotte's Hospital. During the season at Sadler's Wells she also appears as a rabbit in Sara Patrick's *Uncle Remus*.

1934. Commanded by post-card to attend *corps de ballet* rehearsals for *Casse-Noisette*, Peggy appears on stage for the first time in May – as a Snowflake – with a payment of two shillings and sixpence per performance.

Summer finds her promoted to the corps of ballet – the youngest member, and now earning a useful thirty shillings a week. During the International Opera Season at Covent Garden, she appears in scenes of *Schwanda the Bagpiper* and *Turandot* – as well as being a gnome in *The Rhinegold*.

At de Valois' request she looks for a more suitable stage name. Margaret quickly becomes Margot, and she takes the Brazilian family name for a surname. As Margot Fontes, she first dances the Mazurka in Fokine's *Les Sylphides* (right).

No-one can foresee that nearly forty years on Fonteyn will still be delighting audiences with her appearance in *Les Sylphides*... her partner in this instance, Anthony Dowell, being a dazzling product of the school destined to emerge from de Valois' founding company.

Les Sylphides

Margot watching Markova from the group of cygnets in Le Lac des Cygnes. Despite her admiration for Markova, Fonteyn quickly acquires a unique 'line' of her own. Above right, a glimpse forward twenty-five years to the same act of Swan Lake

Margot seated fourth from the right, watching Markova in Giselle

20th March; she takes the rôle of The Young Creole Girl in the revival of Frederick Ashton's *Rio Grande* (right). Markova had originally created the rôle in the Camargo Society's production of the ballet, in 1931.

Rio Grande

Margot continues to watch Markova assiduously, and in her spare moments mourns, with her friend Berenice Marks (Markova's young sister) the sheer impossibility of their ever growing to look like the slim and fragile ballerina who leads them.

From Brazil there now comes disapproval from the head of the Fontes family, who considers theatrical associations highly undesirable publicity for the family name. The girl who is destined to be awarded Brazil's highest civilian honour, the Cruziero do Sul, calmly changes her surname to Fonteyn, having found the name next to Fontes in the London Telephone Directory. Nobody at the time recalls that the first ballerina in Ballet's history is recorded as a certain Mademoiselle La Fontaine. De Valois likes the new name – "more English" – for an English company.

Partnered by William Chappell

Rio Grande

"Only fifteen...it is impossible to say what she may become, but it is certain that here are the makings of a ballerina. 'Anything that a dancer ought to know I can teach' said the old Cecchetti to Pavlova; 'but you have something that cannot be taught; it is born' – It is not too much to say that Margot Fonteyn has in her something of this gift that cannot be taught. With good teaching, grinding work, with devotion to high ideals, there is no saying what this child of fifteen may not do."

Jasper Howlett, "Talking of Ballet"

Rio Grande, 1935 "...her technique has been strengthened and her stage personality has developed. She is able to grip her audience, and provided she continues in the way she has begun and does not grow too tall she should develop into a really great artiste."

"The Sitter Out", The Dancing Times

During the year she takes over (at short notice) the rôle of Papillon in *Carnaval.*

With the departure from the company of Markova, Margot takes over the leading rôle in *Les Rendez-vous* (partnered by Harold Turner) on 27th September, which gives the *Morning Post* a chance to report of the young Fonteyn that she has "some of that intoxicating quality always associated with great dancers."

Les Rendezvous

The Haunted Ballroom

She appears again in de Valois' ballet, this time in the leading rôle of Alicia...

"The Company has produced from its ranks a budding ballerina who looks like blooming with the best. Margot Fonteyn, a sixteen-year-old, already displays the poise, the spirit and the promise of a star."

The Observer

With Robert Helpmann, Julia Farron, Celia Franca

"Truly poetic was the ending – Miss Fonteyn's pitying backward glance at the young heir to the curse…"

Richard Capell
The Daily Telegraph

Façade

1935. She does the Polka in Frederick Ashton's *Façade*. The background cow belongs to two of Gordon Anthony's studio pictures. They are part of a huge portrait series taken by Ninette de Valois' brother during the formative years of the company.

Above, at the centre of the village fête in Le Baiser de la Fée

Left, as guest with the Rambert Ballet Club, in Antony Tudor's Lysistrata, with Walter Gore as her partner

Below, with Frederick Ashton and Elisabeth Schooling in Les Sylphides, for Rambert

Le Baiser de la Fée

After much initial antipathy to the idea, Ashton is finally persuaded by de Valois to choreograph on the young Margot. He is annoyed by her seeming resistance to his choreography, but the young girl is secretly in awe of Ashton and is dismayed by her inability to master his intricate steps. De Valois keeps counsel from the sidelines, and the early incompatability finally resolves itself in a flood of tears from Margot and a new understanding from Ashton.

26th November sees the first Ashton rôle created by Fonteyn – that of the Bride in a ballet to Stravinsky's score, *Le Baiser de la Fée*.

Above, with Pearl Argyle as The Fairy and Harold Turner as the Bridegroom

Le Lac des Cygnes

LONDON NEWS AGENCY

16th December 1935; she essays, for the first time, the rôle of Odette in *Le Lac des Cygnes* (with Ruth French dancing Odile).

Left, first night celebration:
Fonteyn with
Joy Newton
Pamela May
June Brae
Julia Farron
Jean Bedells

ANTHONY

Above, de Valois inspects Margot's Swan Lake tutu. Her first, made by Pavlova's dresser Manya, serves as the model for all subsequent tutus, and the style of all the Sadler's Wells' tutus thereafter derives directly from Margot's original Pavlova model

As Odette in Swan Lake, right and opposite

MERLYN SEVE

1936. On 11th February she creates the rôle of The Woman in the Ball Dress, in Frederick Ashton's newest work *Apparitions*. She is cast as an unattainable ideal of womanhood, first glimpsed at a Ball by a poet suffering from heightened visions induced by laudanum. Ashton devises for Fonteyn a rôle perfectly in keeping with her emerging gifts. Remote yet provocative, she waltzes her way through the activity with a disarming ease. In one brief nightmare scene she takes on an evil and forceful nature before returning to the calm, sad and rather enigmatic personality glimpsed at the end of the ballet. It is a rôle without undue technical traps, perfect for Margot's degree of confidence, and catering to her youthful pleasure in acquired sophistication. Her success in the work is immediate, and it is noted with satisfaction that her subtle qualities are in no way overshadowed by Helpmann's powerful stage presence. He is, in fact, an entirely considerate and encouraging partner to the young girl, despite his eminence in the company and his off-stage remoteness for the younger members.

Apparitions

A semi-dress rehearsal, with Robert Helpmann

The company has been alternating between the Old Vic Theatre and Sadler's Wells Theatre, but during the initial run of *Apparitions,* the company settles permanently at the Wells in Finsbury, North London.

During June–July 1936 Mrs. Hookham chaperones four girls for a second visit to Paris, where they continue lessons with Egorova, Kschessinskaya and Preobrajenska.

Below; the visit to Paris: Margot in the Bois de Boulogne; on the Newhaven-Dieppe boat; and posing for Pamela May's camera (l. to r.) Laurel Martin, Mrs. Hookham, Margot, Molly Brown

Aida

On 22nd September 1936 she dances Petipa's Aurora *pas de deux* for the first time.

In October, she appears as The Slave Girl in the ballet sequence of the opera *Aida* at Covent Garden.

10th November; Ashton's *Nocturne* is premièred.

Nocturne

GORDON ANTHONY

J. W. DEBENHAM

Ashton's choreography for the young girl now veers from the 'Markova' image of sophisticated elegance, to harness instead the softer lyricism and dramatic pathos inherent in his new dancer's work. He casts her as a simple Parisian flower girl, hopelessly in love with a rich man she can never approach. Margot is once more widely acclaimed by the esoteric and opinionated London ballet audience. Her sad simplicity is considered infinitely touching and again Ashton does not risk distressing her with steps that are too difficult, leaving her freedom to take on the emotion of his interpretation of Delius' nocturne *Paris*.

Far left, with Robert Helpmann,
and on this page with Frederick Ashton

During November 1936, at short notice she steps into *Prometheus,* by de Valois.

In December the B.B.C. transmits from Alexandra Palace Studios a television programme in which Margot does the Polka from *Façade,* a remarkably early appearance on the newly inaugurated Service.

On 8th January 1937 there follows her next big classical rôle – the Sugar Plum Fairy in *Casse-Noisette.*

Casse-Noisette

Above, the Sugar Plum Fairy;
and left with Robert Helpmann in Act II

Giselle

with Robert Helpmann

On 19th January 1937 she makes an auspicious début in the historic and challenging rôle of *Giselle*.

Act I

Below and right, 1937. Above, thirty years on

Act II

with Helpmann

Giselle

"He loves me, he loves me not ..."

with Rassine

with Some.

with Nureyev

1965

1937

The constancy of her line is seen in two pictures with twenty-eight years between them. The shadow in the 1937 picture, on the far right, gives a truer view of the angle of the arms

1965

Giselle
The Mad Scene

"...Dame Margot's Mad Scene represents one of the great acting achievements of this or any era – and I'm not exaggerating when I say it would equal the art of a Sarah Bernhardt or a Judith Anderson."

Walter Terry, on *Giselle*
N. Y. Herald Tribune, 9.5.65

FELIX FONTEYN

1937

1937

1946

1964

1960's

R. FALIGANT

At the Paris Opéra with Nureyev

The pas de deux posed here with Harold Turner in his rôle of the Blue Skater

Les Patineurs

16th February 1937. Ashton's new ballet is premièred at the Sadler's Wells Theatre.

Later, on television, with her Adagio partner Robert Helpmann, right

A Wedding Bouquet

On 27th April 1937 she creates the rôle of forlorn Julia in *A Wedding Bouquet*, the delicious saga of a French provincial wedding as told by Gertrude Stein and brilliantly re-interpreted by Ashton – to Miss Stein's great approval.

Julia Farron as the Mexican terrier Pépé

Robert Helpmann as The Bridegroom

In the Spring she dances Columbine in *Carnaval* for the first time.

During June, at the Théâtre des Champs-Elysées for the Paris Exhibition, she dances as a Black Pawn in the première of de Valois' *Checkmate* (billed on this occasion *Echec et Mat*).

16th November; she dances in *Les Rendez-vous* (above and right).

She also appears in a Gala Concert at His Majesty's – "Margot Fonteyn danced most beautifully the 'Aurora' *pas de deux* with Anton Dolin at the concert given in honour of Nijinsky."

21st December 1937; Margot Fonteyn is seen for the first time in both the ballerina rôles of *Le Lac des Cygnes*.

Towards the end of the year she alternates with Pearl Argyle in Ashton's *Pomona*.

At Cambridge (where the Ballet performs for a week at the Arts Theatre) Margot meets a young Panamanian undergraduate Roberto Arias, above, photographed at the time by Leslie Edwards

Pomona

As Odette with Helpmann (above), Somes (centre), and Nureyev (right)

Swan Lake
(Le Lac des Cygnes)

As Odile with Helpmann (left), Somes (centre), and Nureyev (below)

Swan Lake

GORDON ANTHONY

As Odette, in 1935 with Helpmann, and in 1965 with Nureyev, above

As Odile   1943

1968

"At Sadler's Wells last night Margot Fonteyn danced the dual role in the full version of *Swan Lake*... In her case the title *ballerina* is far more than a courtesy. In the many poetical passages she was admirable, but it was only in the virtuoso Act III that she proved herself beyond a doubt. I have never seen her so regal in manner or half so brilliant, in spite of indifferent fouettés and an occasional jerkiness."

Arnold Haskall 22.12.37

Odette, 1937

"The peculiar atmosphere of poetry which infuses the smallest of her movements merged perfectly with the sinister gloom of the second and fourth acts, but in the third, which demands sheer technique and a certain hardness of acting, she rose to it with a stability that one has not seen in her before. If she still lacks something in brilliance of attack, it is probable that the self-consciousness responsible will dissolve as she matures. Last night proved that a young English dancer has genius."

Tangye Lean 22.12.37

Swan Lake

Odile, 1937 and 1953

Swan Lake
with Michael Somes

in Amsterdam

COLL. FONTEYN

HOUSTON ROGERS

Swan Lake

With Helpmann, 1938,
and Somes, 1953, right

Swan Lake
Act III

*With Nureyev, in Japan, 1963,
and New York, 1970, below*

Swan Lake

Choreographic revisions in a new production result in the elimination of the rôle of the Prince's friend Benno.

Above, with Leslie Edwards as Benno and Michael Somes as Siegfried

Left and below, with Rudolf Nureyev as Siegfried

Opposite, with David Wall as Siegfried

In 1938 she takes over Pearl Argyle's rôle of Venus in *Judgement of Paris*, an Ashton work first seen earlier in the year, and one not destined to survive long.

Judgement of Paris

with Helpmann

On 15th April 1938, above, she appears again on the medium of television, in a programme from Bach and Handel

*Preparations for a production of
The Sleeping Princess*

with Michael Somes

Horoscope

27th January 1938; Ashton's *Horoscope,* to a score by Constant Lambert, is premièred at Sadler's Wells.

Horoscope is given again on the first night of the Autumn Season, 18th October.

Pamela May as The Moon, left, and Richard Ellis and Alan Carter as The Gemini

*As "The Young Woman with the Sun in Virgo and the Moon in Leo"
she dances with Michael Somes as "The Young Man with the Sun in
Leo and the Moon in Virgo"*

GORDON ANTHONY

The Sleeping Beauty
(The Sleeping Princess)

On 2nd February 1939 a Charity First Performance of *The Sleeping Princess* is attended by Queen Mary at Sadler's Wells. "Margot Fonteyn . . . gave what was probably the best performance of her career."

The Times 3.2.39

On 16th March a press picture is released with the heading and caption:

"CARRY ON LONDON"

"Despite the trouble in Central Europe, the ballet is busy carrying on with rehearsals at the Royal Opera House, Covent Garden, for the Royal Command Performance to be given in honour of the French President's visit next week."

June Brae and Michael Somes can be seen behind Margot as Aurora – transposed from Act I to the Prologue for the photograph.

FOX PHOTOS

GORDON ANTHONY

GORDON ANTHONY

Act I

with Helpmann

Act II

with Helpmann

GORDON ANTHONY

EDWARD MANDINIAN

Act I

Act II

with Helpmann

The Sleeping Beauty

Second Production

EDWARD MANDINIAN

Act III
with Helpmann

Right, with Ninette de Valois and guests after a performance on the first Sadler's Wells Tour of North America, 1949

COLL FONTEYN

HOUSTON ROGERS

The Sleeping Beauty

MAURICE SEYMOUR

Covent Garden, 1954

ASSOCIATED PRESS

with Robert Helpmann in the Milan Production, 1950

RUDOLF PILNER

with David Paltenghi, Vienna, 1946

in a Japanese production, 1959

1946

1964

The Sleeping Beauty

Arabesques from Act I

Act III pas de deux conclusion, with Helpmann, Somes and Nureyev

Filming Act I of The Sleeping Beauty, 1968, with Adrian Grater as The King. Aurora has been pricked by the spindle

With Mikifumu Nagata,
The Tchaikovsky Memorial Tokyo Ballet,
May, 1973

The Sleeping Beauty

The Royal Ballet restages the entire production in 1969, and again in 1973. Fonteyn dances in the first of these new productions during the New York Season in 1970, and in the second, during the Brazilian Tour of 1973.

With Leslie Edwards and Pamela May as the King and Queen

With Nureyev in Ashton's 1969 Awakening pas de deux

"At the second performance, she was incomparable from start to finish...was so carefree and coltish that there was no doubt at all that one was watching a sixteen-year-old at play. Fonteyn at fifty? Hers is the art, not simply the act, of dancing."

Walter Terry on *The Sleeping Beauty*
Saturday Review 16.5.70

On 22nd March 1939, two acts of *The Sleeping Princess* are given at a Command Performance at Covent Garden for the President of the French Republic. It is then televised from Alexandra Palace on 29th March, above, with Ashton and Chappell among the Princes.

On 27th April, at the première of Ashton's *Cupid and Psyche*, Margot steps in for the indisposed Pamela May, as Ceres, in Scene III.

The Ballet Season ends on 18th May with a further performance of *The Sleeping Princess,* followed by a tour of Cambridge, Oxford, and Bournemouth. Travelling as part and parcel of a touring ballet company, with the constant search for 'digs' in strange towns, now becomes an ingrained aspect of Margot's existence. She goes to Manchester, Liverpool...

Left, on tour with Pamela May and Moyra Fraser; centre with her Great Aunt Purdie; and, right, with Frederick Ashton at the Vic-Wells Ball, 14th March (Margot's costume designed by William Chappell)

...On 3rd September, while the company is in a train, en route to Leeds, war is declared between Great Britain and Germany. Upon arrival in Leeds, the company is peremptorily disbanded. But spurred by her enthusiastic 'lieutenants', Ashton and Lambert, de Valois finally re-calls the company in London. They re-assemble for a tour on the 'co-operative' system, with a basic salary offer of £5 per week – "a colossal sum" writes Margot at this time. They go to Newcastle, Leicester, Leeds, Birmingham, Southsea, Brighton, Cambridge, Nottingham, Glasgow... In London Margot and her mother live in Pelham Place (above). Subsequently, in Pelham Crescent, the windows and doors are blown out by a bomb.

Les Sylphides

The company has returned to Sadler's Wells Theatre. There is no orchestra, only two pianos played with indefatigable verve by Constant Lambert and Hilda Gaunt.

26th December 1939; a revival of *Les Sylphides*.

With Robert Helpmann as The Poet

Dante Sonata

1940. Ashton, in his usual close collaboration with Lambert, produces a new ballet full of significant and contemporary undertones – the struggle of Children of Light against evil Children of Darkness. *Dante Sonata* is premièred on 23rd January at Sadler's Wells.

Somes and Fonteyn, as Children of Light, right.
Below, Fonteyn as a Child of Light, caught by
Helpmann and June Brae as Children of Darkness

FELIX FONTEYN

GORDON ANTHONY/V & A

THE SKETCH

GORDON ANTHONY

J. W. DEBENHAM

The Wise Virgins

On the last night of the Sadler's Wells Season, 27th January 1940, Margot dances *The Sleeping Princess*. The company then tours again for nine weeks, including Cambridge, Hull, Leeds and Sheffield. On the return to Sadler's Wells, and in direct contrast to the anguish of *Dante Sonata*, Ashton now devises a serenely beautiful work to the music of Bach, orchestrated by William Walton. *The Wise Virgins* opens on 24th April.

As The Bride, with Michael Somes as The Bridegroom

During 1940 the company changes its name from the Vic-Wells Ballet to become the Sadler's Wells Ballet. In May, the company is sent to Holland for a week of performances, where the last day coincides with the German invasion. After a protracted and desperate evacuation, minus all scenery, costumes and personal possessions — but with de Valois wearing Ashton's dinner jacket in order to effect its deliverance from the enemy — the exhausted group eventually reaches the relative safety of England on Tuesday, 14th May.

Left, leaving Victoria Station with Mary Honer. Below, an ironically peaceful scene in The Hague (l. to r.) Helpmann, Honer, de Valois, Brae, Fonteyn, Ashton, May. Right, safely back in London

Back in London, they are swiftly organised for a Tour to the West Country, where most of the performances take place in army barracks.

On 23rd July *Façade* is revived, with new sets and costumes (above) by John Armstrong.

Façade

She dances in the Tango with Ashton,
and with Helpmann (opposite page).

95

Nocturne is revived

The Wanderer

On 27th January 1941 she creates the rôle of Success, in Ashton's notable ballet *The Wanderer,* first seen at the New Theatre, London, with décor by Graham Sutherland.

with Robert Helpmann

Orpheus
and
Evridice

28th May 1941; she creates the rôle of Amour, in de Valois' newest ballet.

ALERT

You will be notified by an illuminated sign if an Air Raid Warning has been sounded during the performance—but that does not mean that an air raid will necessarily take place. If you wish to leave for home or an official Air Raid Shelter you are at liberty to do so. All we ask is that—if you feel you must go—you will depart quietly and without excitement.

During Alerts no trains run from Piccadilly Circus to Charing Cross, Waterloo or Elephant; but there are special buses from Haymarket and Jermyn Street.

"Sometimes the bombs would fall, and the warning light would go on at the back of the theatre, and we would hear the crashes getting nearer and nearer. But the extraordinary thing is that no one would ever leave the theatre – we just went on as if nothing was happening."

By the Autumn of 1941, the exhaustive pattern of continual performing is well and truly set. On 11th October Margot can be seen as Princess Aurora at both the matinée *and* the evening performance. This double stint is repeated again on the 25th of the month, when signs of tiredness are visible.

However, for the new season she is busy doing *Casse-Noisette* on Christmas Eve, and again on the 27th; *The Sleeping Princess* on the 29th and *Le Lac des Cygnes* on the 31st. Three nights after all *that* she is again to be found doing two performances on the same day of *The Sleeping Beauty* (partnered by John Hart) and yet described as "radiant and tireless". This is to have a most exact parallel thirty years later in Marseilles, and again in Philadelphia.

In Robert Helpmann's new ballet, premièred 14th January 1942

Comus

Comus

As The Lady, with Robert Helpmann as Comus

Hamlet

19th May 1942; with Ashton taken into the Forces, Helpmann is left in a new dual capacity as leading dancer and choreographer. Following *Comus,* he now constructs a Freudian nightmare, using the Tchaikovsky Hamlet overture. Taking the famous lines, beginning "For in that sleep of death what dreams may come…", he presents the shifting, changing characters that might have crowded the dying Hamlet's brain. Ophelia, at times, becomes a blurred entity strangely like Gertrude.

"Helpmann has done dementia parts for years… He has been carried off the stage for dead more than any other artist in London. Margot Fonteyn has also specialised in delirium."

The Star

The Rake's Progress

December 1942; she appears in the current revival of de Valois' master-piece, as the Betrayed Girl.

Coppélia

Act I

On 23rd January 1943 *Coppélia* is revived at the New Theatre. The ballet, with its famous Delibes score, had been re-created in Imperial Russia in a notable version by Marius Petipa and Enrico Cecchetti. It is their version that is re-created for The Sadler's Wells Ballet by Nicholas Sergeyev, whose invaluable private books of notation, retrieved from Russia at the time of the Revolution, provide the basis for the English revivals of the great Petipa and Ivanov ballets.

Coppélia

*Swanhilda pretending to be the clock-
work doll Coppélia, in Act II. Robert
Helpmann as Dr. Coppelius*

"I have seen Genée and I have seen Lopokova in this first of the
classical doll ballets, and each was, in her way, supreme. But
neither of them surpassed Margot Fonteyn in exquisite precision,
in delicate gaiety, in fresh enchantment and lyrical glamour.
Could the part have been better danced even at its original
performance after no less than three years of rehearsals?

This is the acme of comedy. And Margot Fonteyn is only 24."

Herbert Farjeon, *Sunday Graphic*

Act II

Act III, with Alexis Rassine as Franz

With Robert Helpmann as St. George

The Quest

On 7th April 1943 she creates Una in Ashton's *The Quest* at the New Theatre. The ballet has a scenario by Doris Langley Moore based on Spenser's *Faerie Queene* with music by Walton.

From 28th June to 3rd July she appears with the Company in open air performances at Victoria Park, Hackney, appearing in *Casse-Noisette* Act III and other single-act works.

The following month she is taken ill, and does not appear again until 7th September, when she dances in the revival of *Le Lac des Cygnes* with new décor by Leslie Hurry.

7th December; she takes over the lead in *Promenade*, at short notice, for the London opening of de Valois' newest ballet

Le Spectre de la Rose

Fonteyn and Rassine against the scenery by Rex Whistler who had also done the superb décor for The Rake's Progress and The Wise Virgins

On 1st February 1944 Fokine's *Le Spectre de la Rose* is revived at the New Theatre, with Fonteyn as The Girl, and Alexis Rassine as The Spectre.

"Margot was exquisite in the dance that she does in her sleep – like a feather lulling a little wind to rest. It has given me that strange elation which a piece of great artistry always fills me with. She is a very great artist – I think the most entirely satisfying one in the theatre at the moment."

Jill Furse, from a letter quoted by Laurence Whistler in *The Initials in The Heart*

There are a number of distractions at this time. On 27th June some unsteadiness in her performance of *Le Lac des Cygnes* is put down to the fact that her home has been bombed the previous evening. Ten days before this, she and Helpmann have done a performance of *Lac* against heavy and continual gun-fire, as well as the rattle of 'doodle-bugs' marking their sinister passage overhead.

However another performance of the Swan classic on the 29th finds her Odette/Odile restored to its usual impeccable steadiness, this time despite continual explosions in the neighbourhood, of the dreaded flying-bombs. But by 5th July some experts detect signs of exhaustion in Act III! The flying-bomb which comes down in Pelham Crescent kills nine people opposite her home, but Margot is still at the theatre when it falls. The gay impression she makes in *Carnaval* in the Autumn is indicative of her recuperative powers.

10th October 1944, *Carnaval* is revived at the Prince's Theatre:
    "Margot Fonteyn's Columbine is a dainty rogue. Her entrance
and oft' repeated runs *sur les pointes* when encircled by the
loving arms of Harlequin, immediately sets the key-note of her
portrayal of the tender, gay love of youth with its fun and joy.
It is a scintillating performance and one that will enhance her
reputation as one of the most versatile and brilliant of artistes."
The Dancing Times

Carnaval

With Alexis Rassine as Harlequin and Gordon Hamilton as Pantaloon

ENSA Tour 1945

In 1945 she joins an ENSA Tour to Paris and Brussels.

On the way to morning class: l. to r. Moira Shearer, Alexis Rassine, Margot, Tom Douglas (Douglas Steuart), Pamela May, Elizabeth Kennedy, Eric Hyrst

Work weariness

With Pamela May and Frederick Ashton, leaving Oslo

European Tour 1946

Below, with Ninette de Valois and Pamela May in Hanover Street, prior to departure for Vienna

20th February 1946; there is a Gala Re-opening of the Royal Opera House at Covent Garden, with a new production of *The Sleeping Princess*, now renamed *The Sleeping Beauty*. The Royal Family attend the performance. It is the beginning of a new era for Covent Garden.

24th April 1946, Ashton's masterwork *Symphonic Variations* is given for the first time.

Symphonic Variations

Cast: Margot Fonteyn, Pamela May, Moira Shearer, Michael Somes, Henry Danton, Brian Shaw

SEQUENCE BARON

During the summer of 1946 there are visits to Vienna, Brussels, Prague, Warsaw, Poznan, Malmö and Oslo.

12th June; she dances with Alexis Rassine in the company's first Covent Garden performance of *Giselle* (left). She dances the first Covent Garden production of *Swan Lake,* with Helpmann, 19th December.

She also appears in Lewis Gilbert's film *The Little Ballerina,* playing 'herself' (below).

12th November; she appears in Ashton's latest offering *Les Sirènes* (opposite). The ballet's frivolities are thought by the newer Covent Garden audience to be too light-hearted for the dignified surroundings of the Opera House. The work is soon dismissed.

Les Sirènes

as La Bolero

with Leslie Edwards

with Robert Helpmann and Frederick Ashton

116

with Robert Helpmann

The Fairy Queen

12th December 1946; Fonteyn and Somes appear as Spirits of the Air in Ashton's ballet sequence for *The Fairy Queen* – a return to the cool classicism Ashton displayed in *Symphonic Variations*, and thus more to the post-war audiences' liking.

with Michael Somes

SEQUENCE GORDON ANTHONY

Le Tricorne

16th February 1947; Massine revives his *Le Tricorne* for Covent Garden, himself dancing with Fonteyn.

Soon after the première of *Le Tricorne*, Margot is away ill for nine weeks, and thus misses the première of the next Massine ballet, *La Boutique Fantasque*, in which she was to have danced the Can-Can.

As The Miller's Wife   *with John Hart*

with Leonide Massine

By the autumn of 1947 she is dancing fully again, and is ready for the third of Massine's revivals for Sadler's Wells Ballet. It is *Mam'zelle Angot,* premièred on 26th November.

Mam'zelle Angot

With Alexander Grant as The Barber, above,
Moira Shearer as The Aristocrat, and
John Hart as The Government Official, left

with Moira Shearer

With Michael Somes as The Caricaturist

Scènes de Ballet

11th February 1948; the première of Ashton's *Scènes de Ballet* (above), at the time an underrated work, but one destined to survive well.

After a week's visit to Holland, in March, the company prepares for a revised production of *Le Lac des Cygnes* in which Fonteyn is to be partnered by Michael Somes. On 13th April the partnership is received with great enthusiasm in the ballet. But the accumulative strain of eight years of ceaseless work for the company suddenly empties the reserves of Fonteyn's stamina. In an overwrought state, she asks the director for leave. Miss de Valois gives her leading dancer three months holiday which she spends in Paris…

…though hardly at rest, for in Paris Roland Petit creates a new ballet for her at the Théâtre Marigny. She plays Agatha, the cat-woman, in *Les Demoiselles de la Nuit,* partnered by Petit (right). The ballet is premièred on 22nd May.

During the last minutes of the *répétition générale,* attended by both Press and public, the massive structure of the set slowly collapses beneath the dancers. But a determined cat-woman emerges from the wreckage and completes the ballet. The evening is rated a huge success!

During the Paris season, in costume by Balmain, Margot also appears in extracts from *The Sleeping Beauty.*

Les Demoiselles de la Nuit

ANGUS MCBEAN

ANGUS MCBEAN

FELIX FONTEYN

Don Juan

25th November 1948; Ashton's ballet is premièred.

"Fonteyn glowed like a black diamond with all the magnificence of style of a centuries-old tradition of dance… She was a jewelled fire."

"…was touched with superlative art."

"…glowed with that flash of limb, that burnished brilliance, that steely precision, and perfect 'school' which is the attribute of the rare artist."

Such critical euphoria gives no clue to the fact that Margot has injured herself during the opening performance. She is sent to hospital, where her leg is put in plaster for six weeks. Moira Shearer will take her place for the first performance of *Cinderella*. Disconsolate, Margot leaves for Paris rather than remain in London and not be dancing. The weeks drag by for her…

As "La Morte Amoureuse", with Robert Helpmann and Moira Shearer, top right

At the end of the summer Margot begins work on *Don Juan*, Ashton's newest ballet, as well as his first three-act ballet, *Cinderella*, which is in preparation.

21st September finds her back in Paris, this time with the company during its two-week season at the Théâtre des Champs-Elysées, in which Fonteyn appears in *Scènes de Ballet*, *Symphonic Variations* and *Le Lac des Cygnes*, to the great approval of her 'new' French audience. In Dusseldorf a week later, the company is equally successful, *Symphonic Variations* continuing to be recognised as an international masterpiece.

COLL FONTEYN

With Moira Shearer in Edinburgh

No pumpkin coach. Leaving St.Bartholomew's Hospital with her leg in plaster; 26th November

Eventually, she dances *Cinderella* for the first time on 25th February 1949.

Cinderella

Fonteyn's early trips to Paris promote a keen interest in good clothes. The innate flair she shows in their wearing is ultimately to result in her election to America's "Fashion Hall of Fame".

Above, for Vogue

...and in her own style, with Yvette Chauviré at Covent Garden, below

FELIX FONTEYN

Modelling clothes for a book on fashion

EDWARD MANDINIAN

COLL. PAMELA MAY

On 10th May 1949, in a pot-pourri of costumes, she performs, with Harold Turner and Michael Somes, a TV programme of popular Ashton successes: *Baiser de la Fée*, *Fairy Queen* and *The Lord of Burleigh pas de trois*.

There is also a revival of *Apparitions* at Covent Garden, dressed by Cecil Beaton. Along with the new costumes a slightly new profile is noticed as well.

During May, she also appears with the Company at the Teatro Communale in Florence.

In June she dances in Copenhagen with Robert Helpmann. At the supper given in her honour after the Command Performance, she tells Helpmann that she will positively not make a speech. Helpmann announces to the guests "Miss Fonteyn is too moved to speak," whereupon Miss Fonteyn gets up and speaks for six minutes.

In Cecil Beaton's costume for
Apparitions

In the Lord of Burleigh
pas de trois for television

129

In New York they are met at the airport by Sol Hurok and by the American ballerina Norah Kaye, above. Left to right David Webster (General Administrator, Covent Garden), Leslie Edwards, Robert Helpmann, Norah Kaye, Frederick Ashton with Margot and Sol Hurok

Throughout the Summer, preparations go ahead for the Company's first visit to North America, under the aegis of the impresario Sol Hurok, who has become enamoured of the Sadler's Wells Ballet, and of Margot Fonteyn, at his first viewing in 1946.

It is a nerve-racking time for everybody, and particularly for Margot, on whom so much depends. She is convinced that her style of dancing will in no way appeal to the new audiences. With trepidation, the Company embarks for New York on 1st October. In New York they are met at the airport by Sol Hurok, and by the American ballerina Nora Kaye.

Margot is photographed in her dressing room (right) before the opening performance of *The Sleeping Beauty* (9th October) during which New Yorkers take the Sadler's Wells Ballet, and particularly its prima ballerina, to their hearts. The following morning a New York paper announces her as "the world's only valid legend".

Margot sends a telegram to her mother: "We seem to have made it."

The departure . . .

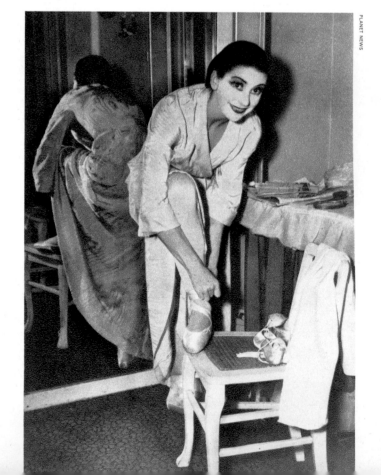

…and the return, the 16th December, wiser, wearier, but infinitely more successful

SADLER'S WELLS prima ballerina Margot Fonteyn awoke today in her suite overlooking New York's Central Park and read that she had captured American hearts.

For an hour before curtaintime no traffic moved in four streets surrounding the Opera House. When the curtain went up, every one of the theatre's 3459 seats was filled, and people were standing eight-deep underneath the famous Diamond Horseshoe from the footlights to the rear entrances.

Margot Fonteyn was a revelation. She has always been able to rise to occasions, but this time she surpassed herself. I have never seen her dance with such technical command or such control of the audience. Burst after burst of applause rolled out from the audience, and after the Rose Adagio a full-throated shout of acclaim went forth. I learned later that all through the cinema appearances that preceeded the American tour she found time to practise the Rose Adagio for two hours every day with her cavaliers. She danced throughout as if dancing were as natural as walking. These were not complex steps as she wove them together, to be cheered as feats of virtuosity. She made the difficult appear unforced, and her great elegance has never been shown to better advantage. Her timing was unbelievably good as she drew the audience along with her to climax after climax. The one word for her performance is " great."

On New York streets, rows of *Time* decorate each magazine stall. The Face of the Week is Fonteyn; the trappings of fame have arrived, almost literally, overnight. One reporter tries gallantly to report on the new phenomenon:

"It comes as a surprise that an English girl named Margot Fontaine is probably the best ballet dancer in the world."

Robert Sylvester
New York Daily News

The New York critics had braced themselves, before the opening, for something well-meaning but artistically less than exquisite. Suffice it to say that this morning all the critics are where the audience was last night—on their knees salaaming and begging the hand of Margot Fonteyn in marriage.

Margot Fonteyn, prima ballerina of the company, danced Aurora as we have never seen it danced before. All that talk about Fonteyn's being a cold dancer is so much bosh.

Here is a ballerina with a God given talent, a perceptive sense of the theatre and a superb technique. Her acting is plain or charged, as the situation requires, her dancing is breath-taking without resort to tricks, mugging and that " watch me now " approach of some of the ballerinas we have been seeing in recent years.

Simple and unaffected, as true greatness always is, Fonteyn knows no apparent limitation in technique. What is more, her technical accomplishments on the stage clearly indicate that she is not exhausting her resources, that she has a tremendous reserve of power and technique beyond that which she is allowing us to see.

She holds an arabesque or an attitude as long as she wishes to, not as long as she can. When she gets off pointe, one has the distinct feeling that she could have stayed longer were it necessary. Similarly, in pirouettes she does as many as she wants to and stops, sharply, clearly, exactly—because she wants to stop not because she has to.

This truly balletic approach to technique—as a means, not an end in itself—gives Fonteyn the possibility of making difficult things look easy, the supreme accomplishment of a real artist.

Fonteyn has elevation and ballon, aplomb and speed, an exquisite style and an elegant manner. Essays, or perhaps sonnets, could be written about her back, so classically straight in turns, poses and lifts, yet so flexible and yielding when the occasion demands. Her legs sing out the beautiful phrases she is dancing and her head, radiant and demure at the same time, crowns a body designed by nature for the ballet.

Walter Terry of *The New York Herald Tribune* said:

' The Sadler's Wells has, let it be said, more than spectacle to offer. It is enormously aristocratic even to the point of leisureliness and its dancers are meticulous, also to the point of leisurely execution, but it . . . has manner, grand manner, and this is a quality we do not always find in our own ballet. As it should have been, the star of the evening was the company's prima ballerina, Margot Fonteyn. She is a lovely dancer, light as down in aerial movements, clean and sharp in the delineation of body lines and precise in the accomplishing of miniature steps and gestures.

' But the admirable policy of having no stars can go only so far; when a star of the first magnitude appears before our eyes, it makes no earthly difference how she is billed. Margot Fonteyn is unmistakably such star, a ballerina among ballerinas. London has known this for some time, Europe has found it out and last night she definitely conquered another continent.'

People at intermission discussing the charm and conviction of the miming. A lady saying of Fonteyn ' Such a lovely child !', completely believing Fonteyn's subtle delineation of the young Aurora on her first appearance.

Margot Fonteyn, in the title role, scored her own personal triumph. Dancing with superb artistry, dazzling precision and balance, and a beautiful freedom of movement which makes the arbitrary conventions of the classic ballet seem her natural element, she captivated the audience from the moment of her first appearance. She was accorded an ovation on her entrance and after each variation, while following the *pas de deux*, danced with Robert Helpmann in the final scene, the audience fairly roared its approval, holding up the performance for a considerable length of time.

The evening was one of the warmest of New York's Indian summer, but the stifling heat did not prevent the New Yorkers from giving her a tumultuous reception. And at the end the tiny figure of the ballerina, standing on the great stage, dominated the whole auditorium, and the gold curtain rose and fell twenty times.

Margot Fonteyn gave an inspired performance which had the whole audience cheering from the Rose Adagio onwards.

Their plaudits were for Margot Fonteyn, who had just convinced them that she was the world's greatest living ballerina.

It was the performance of Fonteyn's career.

Cheers rose to a crescendo as prima ballerina Margot Fonteyn acknowledged her ovations.

With Helpmann in the last act they stopped the show again. It seemed a fitting tribute to the 14-year-old partnership of Fonteyn, Helpmann and Constant Lambert, the conductor, a partnership unprecedented in ballet.

The *New York Times* said she was a star of the first magnitude, adding: " She is young and lovely to look at. She has technical equipment so strong she seems to ignore it."

Hurok, the great ballet impresario of America, who first brought Anna Pavlova over to the States, says of her. " Margot has no equal among the ballerinas of the world."

To see Miss Fonteyn is a privilege.

"Oh to be in England now that Fonteyn's there," paraphrases Irving Kolodin in the New York press, after the Sadler's Wells Ballet returns home.

In Paris, working with Olga Preobrajenska again

Don Quixote

On 20th February 1950 she plays the Lady Dulcinea, and Aldonza, in de Valois' new ballet *Don Quixote* at the start of the London season.

As Aldonza, with Robert Helpmann as The Don

As Dulcinea, right

Above, with Helpmann during a visit to Norway, 30th January–2nd February 1950. Below, with President Auriol of France, after the Covent Garden Gala in which Fonteyn dances in Symphonic Variations and The Sleeping Beauty Act III

Ballet Imperial

On 5th April 1950 Balanchine mounts his *Ballet Imperial* for the Sadler's Wells Ballet. Margot does not find herself totally at ease in the new idiom and Balanchine subsequently wastes no opportunity to criticise the English 'Lyrical' school, and Ashton and Fonteyn in particular.

On 8th April Fonteyn, Helpmann and May appear as guests in a production of *The Sleeping Beauty*, at La Scala, Milan.

With Michael Somes in Ballet Imperial

On 15th May there is a 21st Anniversary Gala for The Sadler's Wells Ballet (it is subsequently discovered to be only the 19th Anniversary). In the performance, Fonteyn dances again the first of her solo rôles with the company: The Young Treginnis in *The Haunted Ballroom* (below), when this photograph is taken. She also appears in *A Wedding Bouquet* and *Façade*.

With Balanchine, before the première

136

With Robert Helpmann in Ile des Sirènes

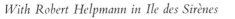

Ile des Sirènes

During June of 1950 she undertakes with Helpmann an English Provincial Tour nicknamed "The Fonteyn Follies". They dance Alfred Rodrigues' *Ile des Sirènes*; also *Les Rendezvous* and *Coppélia* (below).

"Were the British dock-worker as concentrated in the pursuit of his art as Miss Margot Fonteyn is in hers, not a few of our present troubles would be unloaded."

Collie Knox, *The Sketch*
28th February 1951

On 4th September 1950 the Sadler's Wells Ballet returns to New York for another four-month tour in America and Canada. Left to right de Valois, Fonteyn, Shearer, Ashton, Somes, and conductor Irving

Daphnis and Chloë

On 5th April 1951, Ashton's *Daphnis and Chloë* is premièred at Covent Garden. A slow starter in the repertoire, it nevertheless allows Margot to give one of her most appealing portrayals in a rôle that comes to be totally associated with her image.

with Alexander Grant as The Pirate Chief

with Michael Somes as Daphnis

On 7th June 1951 she is made a Commander of the British Empire in the King's Birthday Honours list. She subsequently travels to Greece for the first time, where she discovers the timeless echoes she has already sensed in Ashton's choreography for *Daphnis and Chloë*.

On 9th July the new Ashton/Lambert collaboration, *Tiresias*, is premièred to very mixed notices from critics currently concerned that no slightest blemish shall escape notice. Fonteyn's long *pas de deux* with John Field is considered a notable highlight in the work, which is otherwise rated over-long and rather dull.

Disappointed in the reception, the Company leaves for the Edinburgh Festival, where *Tiresias* (commissioned by The Arts Council for the Festival of Britain in 1951), is to be performed again. After their arrival, they are stunned to hear that Constant Lambert has died suddenly in London. The Company has lost a most treasured colleague.

It is a difficult time. Soon after this Margot strains a foot and is absent from dancing for the remainder of the year.

Tiresias

*With
scenario
and score
by Constant
Lambert*

As the female Tiresias with her lover (John Field)

As Sylvia, leader of Diana's huntresses

With Michael Somes as Aminta and Alexander Grant as the Statue of Eros, Act I

During April 1952 Margot appears at the San Carlos Theatre, Lisbon, and at the Rivoli Theatre, Oporto.

On 8th June she appears in Paris, for a Gala Performance in aid of the Restoration of the Palace of Versailles.

In July she is in Rome; then Capri.

During the Summer she is pictured in mosaic (alongside Winston Churchill) in the floor of the National Gallery in London.

On 3rd September 1952 Ashton's 3-Act version of *Sylvia* is premièred.

Working with Vera Volkova in Copenhagen

Act II, Orion's Grotto

Sylvia

Act III

Diphtheria

On 28th September 1952, at the Städtische Oper International Festival in Berlin, she dances in *Giselle* and *Daphnis and Chloë*, and in the first two weeks of October she appears in *Coppélia* – at Croydon.

On 8th November, in Southampton, a bright young doctor correctly diagnoses Margot's apparent acute sore throat as diphtheria, and she is hospitalised immediately. Her recovery is slow and the illness leaves her in a seriously weakened state. The after-effects are far more alarming than the general public is allowed to know. There is some localised paralysis in her legs, feet and also mouth. Walking is a hazardous operation based on guess-work, and her speech is barely decipherable, but friends are amazed to find that she can still discover humour in her strange situation.

On 18th December she appears, walking determinedly with Frederick Ashton to see the première of a new production of *Le Lac des Cygnes* (left), but it is noticed by others in the audience that she looks disturbingly pale and listless. Her legion of admirers becomes greatly alarmed when her projected return has to be cancelled "indefinitely" by the Box Office.

Practising a far from strenuous rôle in *Apparitions,* she finds she has almost no energy to complete even the simplest of movements, but by March 1953 she is feeling slightly more confident (below). Her return is now billed for 18th March.

Fonteyn's eventual return to the stage (in *Apparitions*) is one of the more remarkable evenings in the history of Covent Garden. At the conclusion of the ballet, the emotional response by the audience, including those who have suddenly crowded into the back of the theatre, is almost overwhelming.

The House continues to call for its favourite artist long after the stage has been covered from wing to wing in floral tributes. The great measure of joy and relief at the return of the audience's darling is summed up by one particular incident:

The General Administrator being observed to have tears streaming down his face (in common with many others on this particular evening) is asked "What on earth is the matter?" to which he replies: "If you don't understand you certainly don't deserve to be told."

Reluctant to speak, Fonteyn finally steps to the front of the stage and says simply: "I don't feel I deserve any of this, but thank you, all of you, very much."

Fonteyn's return to the stage: photographed after Apparitions

Homage to The Queen

Premièred on Coronation Night, 2nd June 1953. Fonteyn has already danced in Act II of Swan Lake with Helpmann who has returned for the special occasion

With Michael Somes rehearsing one of Ashton's lifts

Homage to The Queen

As Queen of the Air with her Consort

In Spain in early July she dances a series of *pas de deux* with Michael Somes, as well as dancing informally in the gypsy caves.

13th September sees the opening of the third North American Tour, with Fonteyn in *Le Lac des Cygnes,* partnered by Somes. The New York performances occur during a severe heatwave.

The Tour continues until January 1954, when Fonteyn and Somes appear in the *Homage pas de deux* on the Ed. Sullivan T.V. Show. The huge, non ballet-minded audience is also intrigued to see scenes from Ashton's *Les Patineurs.* The dancing is rated a particular success for the programme.

L'Entrée de Madame Butterfly

On 31st May 1954 with Michael Somes, she begins a series of guest appearances in *Le Lac des Cygnes* in Belgrade, with the Yugoslav National Ballet.

On 17th June she dances *Le Lac des Cygnes* in Holland, as well as *Homage to The Queen* and *The Sleeping Beauty* Act III.

On 27th June 1955 she appears in the gardens of the Alhambra Palace, Granada, for a Music Festival. Included in the programme is a new solo by Ashton, *L'Entrée de Madame Butterfly,* with a costume by Christian Dior (top right).

5th July 1954; de Valois persuades Fonteyn to accept the Presidency of the Royal Academy of Dancing on the retirement of her predecessor, Dame Adeline Genée Isitt, left

Returning from Holland, far left

Honorary Degrees

Litt. D. Leeds, 14th May 1953

"I am probably the most illiterate ballerina you have ever seen."

Mus. D. London, 26th November 1954

LL. D. Edinburgh, 5th July 1963.
   Because she is unable to attend their ceremony for the second year running, Edinburgh make a most unusual exception to the general rule: her Honorary Doctorate of Laws is granted *in absentia*.

Left, walking with the Lord Archbishop of York in procession. Cambridge 1962

LL. D. Manchester, 18th February 1966

LL. D. Cambridge, 14th June 1962

Mus. D. Oxford, 24th June 1959

KEYSTONE

DAILY HERALD

ASSOCIATED NEWSPAPERS

MIKE DAVIS

HOUSTON ROGERS

The Firebird

Below, Karsavina rehearsing Fonteyn and Somes

SCOTSMAN FEATURES

NUGENT STUDIOS

Edinburgh, August 1954.
Karsavina coaches Fonteyn and Somes in *The Firebird,* for the revival of the Fokine/Stravinsky ballet, now being remounted by the Sadler's Wells Ballet. The production is premièred under difficult conditions at the Edinburgh Festival on 23rd August, with the orchestra conducted by Ernest Ansermet.

The ballet opens (with better stage conditions) in London on 31st August, again conducted by Ansermet. Fonteyn has a huge personal triumph in the notoriously difficult Firebird rôle. Her mastery of every nuance is considered absolute.

with Michael Somes as Prince Ivan

The Firebird

153

Greece

Retrospective Interlude

China

Attention to detail in 1935...

... and 1966

Opening an art exhibition 1948...

...and 1968

On the day before her wedding she dances as The Firebird at the matinée on the 5th February, and as Chloë at the evening performance. In the finale of *Daphnis and Chloë* the 'villagers' enter with their scarves full of confetti and rose petals. There are streamers from the audience and another emotional outpouring towards a greatly loved artist (left).

Margot says to her audience "If I am one-tenth as happy in my future life as I am tonight I shall be a very lucky girl. I thank you from the bottom of my heart for all your kind wishes."

The eve of her wedding

On 27th September 1954 the Sadler's Wells Ballet opens a two week exchange season at the Paris Opéra, with Fonteyn in *The Sleeping Beauty*. The Paris audience is far from astonished by the production, but it greets Margot herself with rapture.

After the Paris season, an exciting Italian tour precedes the company's provincial tour of England in the autumn.

1955. While in America touring with the company, Margot is courted by a United Nations representative who appears initially during the interval of a performance. It is the same 'Tito' Arias from Cambridge days. The worldly, world-famous ballerina and the sophisticated diplomat slowly re-discover the same elements of personality in each other that had marked their fleeting encounters those fifteen years earlier.

In London, Margot calls a Press Conference (which she manages on her own) and announces her impending marriage in Paris, planned for a gap in her dancing schedule which, she considers, will continue "for ever". Once the news is made public there is great excitement, and more than a little wistfulness, from her admirers beyond the footlights.

On 6th February she arrives in Paris (above) for the civil wedding ceremony in the Panamanian Consulate. The reception is held in the lilac-filled salon of the Plaza Athenée Hotel. The day is one of total confusion, compounded by numbers of pressmen fighting to get a clear view of the bride, in her Dior dress of silver grey paper-taffeta and her feathered head-dress.

Later, Margot arranges a party and cabaret after the ballet for her friends and colleagues at the Opera House. Under a marquee erected on the stage, Margot, wearing her wedding dress, dances with her husband (right) and then in turn with all the other male guests.

1956. The Arias household has much to celebrate at this time. It is announced that Dr. Arias will be the new Panamanian Ambassador to the Court of St. James, while in the New Year's Honours List Fonteyn features as a D.B.E. – the first dancer to win such an award while still in mid-career. As a designate Dame of the British Empire she appears on the 2nd January in *Swan Lake* at Covent Garden, and four nights later is to be seen in her old setting of the Sadler's Wells Theatre, during a Gala celebrating its re-opening. A week later, Winston Churchill sees Fonteyn in one of his favourite settings: the Monte Carlo Casino. With Somes she is a guest with the London Festival Ballet.

On 23rd January she appears in the Pavlova Midnight Gala at Covent Garden, as Queen of the Air in an extract from *Homage to The Queen*.

In The Firebird at Milan on the 10th March 1955, a modified head-dress is tried for the occasion

In Les Sylphides with John Gilpin while guest with the Festival Ballet at Monte Carlo, Christmas 1955

Outside Buckingham Palace after her investiture by H. M. Queen Elizabeth The Queen Mother on 7th February

Dr. Arias and his wife leave their home after the news of his appointment as Ambassador

La Péri

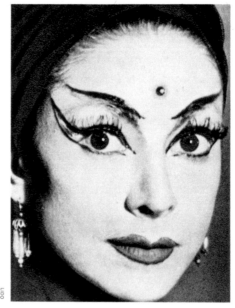

On 15th February the première of Ashton's newest version of the Péri legend takes place – his first having been in 1931 for Markova and himself.

The Persian fable tells of the beautiful fallen angel barred from Paradise for a period of penance, and how Iskender the Shah steals from her the lotus of immortality, which promptly glows ruby red, betraying his desires…

With Michael Somes as Iskender

La Péri

On 19th February 1956 she appears with the Sadler's Wells Ballet on television, dancing in *Aurora's Wedding,* to mark the tenth anniversary of the re-opening of the Opera House. Despite the obscure nature of the anniversary it is in fact almost the twentieth anniversary of Fonteyn's first appearance on television, a medium she graces spasmodically throughout her career.

On 29th February, partnered by Michael Somes, she begins five guest appearances with the Norwegian Ballet Company in Oslo.

On 22nd March London sees *L'Entrée de Madame Butterfly* (billed as *Entrée Japonaise*) at a Covent Garden Gala.

HOUSTON ROGERS

On 12th April, Fonteyn and Somes make the first of four appearances with the Finnish National Ballet in Helsinki dancing in *Swan Lake* and *The Sleeping Beauty*.

From Helsinki they go straight to Nice, to appear with the Festival Ballet, and the following night dance *Swan Lake* in Monte Carlo for the occasion of Prince Rainier's marriage to Miss Grace Kelly.

On 5th May there is yet another Gala Performance at Covent Garden, this one of some importance, for it celebrates the 25th anniversary of the Sadler's Wells Ballet. The highlight of the programme is the first performance of Ashton's *pièce d'occasion*, *Birthday Offering*.

In the Gala, Fonteyn appears in The Tango from Façade, with Helpmann…

…and with Michael Somes in the new Ashton ballet, a glittering neo-classical exercise designed to show off the various talents of the company's leading dancers

Birthday Offering

In October, Fonteyn and Somes make guest appearances during the Johannesburg Festival. An extra performance of *Swan Lake Act II* is arranged for an audience of 6,000 – in pouring rain, at Zoo Lake.

In November the projected visit by Sadler's Wells to Russia is cancelled, due to current political tension.

On 31st December Fonteyn appears in Milan, in *Casse-Noisette*.

On 16th January 1957 the Sadler's Wells Ballet receives a Royal Charter and becomes henceforth The Royal Ballet.

Petrushka

On 26th March she appears in the rôle of The Doll Ballerina in the Covent Garden revival of Fokine's *Petrushka,* reproduced for The Royal Ballet by Diaghilev's régisseur Serge Grigoriev and his wife, Lubov Tchernicheva.

On 17th May with Michael Somes, Rowena Jackson and Bryan Ashbridge, she leaves for a guest season in Australia with the Borovansky Ballet. Fonteyn dances *Swan Lake* Act II, the *Casse-Noisette pas de deux,* and *The Sleeping Beauty.*

On 1st September she arrives in New York for the Company's fifth tour, and opens the season in *The Sleeping Beauty* on 8th September. The stagehands at the Metropolitan Opera House, where she has been known to them by the nickname of "Dimples", now show their respect by referring to her as "Dame Dimples".

The painting by Pietro Annigoni, of Fonteyn in traditional Panamanian costume, is hung in the Arias' ambassadorial residence. The picture has been exhibited in the same Royal Academy Exhibition which has displayed Maurice Lambert's statue of the assoluta

Cinderella for American television. Above, rehearsing in New York, with Ashton in costume for one of the ugly sisters, and the director of the transmission, Clark Jones

Watching Ashton attend to detail

Cinderella is recorded for British television; with Somes as the Prince, below

London, 1958

With her niece Lavinia, 1959

With Children

After 19 curtain calls at a handicapped children's matinée.
Australia, 1957

America, 1960

Brazil, 1960

Johannesburg, 1971

Presented to H.M. The Queen

On 24th March 1958 Dr. Arias resigns his ambassadorship.

On 27th March Fonteyn dances the *Casse-Noisette pas de deux* for a Royal Ballet Benevolent Fund Gala.

On 10th June she dances in *Birthday Offering* at a Gala Performance for the 100th Anniversary of the Covent Garden Opera House, attended by H.M. The Queen and H.R.H. Prince Philip, Duke of Edinburgh (left).

On 29th August Fonteyn dances at the Paris Opéra, followed by a tour of Manchester, Bristol and Oxford with The Royal Ballet.

During September and October, Frederick Ashton creates the three-act ballet *Ondine* as a vehicle for Fonteyn.

On 27th October *Ondine* is premièred at Covent Garden.

Ashton rehearsing Fonteyn as Ondine and Michael Somes as Palemon

Opposite, with Royal Academy of Dancing students, 1961

Ondine the water sprite

Ondine

Ondine's dance with her shadow

Ondine with her shadow

Ondine

with Michael Somes

"*Ondine* was fashioned for Margot. It shows her as she herself: humble, loving, exquisite, enchanting; in short, Margot Fonteyn."

Marie Rambert

Ondine

The marriage of Ondine and Palemon; with Leslie Edwards as The Hermit

The shipwreck scene

Ondine tries to avoid giving Palemon the fatal kiss

Ashton's choice of the story of Ondine for Fonteyn's signature ballet is an astute one, for the sea appears as a strong element throughout her life.

An ondine in the South of France

On 29th November she goes to Munich for one week; then on 21st December she appears as the Sugar Plum Fairy in a television presentation of *Casse-Noisette*.

Prior to dancing engagements in Japan, she films *Ondine, Swan Lake Act II* and *The Firebird,* and then announces "I would never make another film!"

Casse-Noisette, on television, with Somes

in Kyoto

SAITO

COLL. FONTEYN

in Tokyo

On 18th February 1959 she arrives in Japan with Michael Somes to begin guest appearances in Tokyo, Kyoto, Nagoya, and Takalazuka.

Fonteyn and Somes later join up with the Touring Section of The Royal Ballet, making appearances in Sydney, Christchurch, Wellington, and Auckland.

On 8th April 1959 she flies via New York to Panama for a "holiday". At midnight on 20th April she is arrested by Panamanian authorities and placed in jail, held on a charge of complicity in revolutionary activities instigated by her husband. Around the world, newspaper headlines show a frantic interest in a "revolution" comprising one fishing boat and a few rifles.

COLL. FONTEYN

As search goes on for ballerina's husband

FONTEYN TURNS UP

Warrant is out for her, says Panama

IAN AITKEN

press reporter on the spot, flew 2,289 miles from New York to
ama and arrived just as the name of Dame Margot Fonteyn's
band, Dr. Roberto Arias, began to be associated with reports of
Here, in his second despatch,
y tells how Fonteyn landed from a fishing launch at dawn
yesterday while the hunt for her husband intensified.

PANAMA CITY, Monday

T was issued by Panama tonight containing
against Dame Margot Fonteyn. This was
the district attorney, Senor Francisco
Fonteyn—centre-piece in allegations of
volutionary plotting—stepped ashore in

THE STRANGEST ROLE SHE'S EVER PLAYED...

MARGOT FLIES OUT SMILING, SILENT

Daily Mail 23/4/59

I don't know where my husband is she says

From STANLEY BURCH
New York, Wednesday.

DAME MARGOT FON-
TEYN, wreathed in
smiles and mystery, flew
into New York today from
Panama City where she
had spent 24 hours in jail.

No, she told a claimouring
crowd as she
swarmed her...

DEDICATION

By HILDA HOOKHAM

CHARM

CONTENT

SUCH FEUDIN' behind the Fonteyn affair

ROBERTO ARIAS
Loves adventure

At the root
of Panama's
troubles is
a family hate as bitter
as in the Montague and
Cap...

MARGOT IN JAIL

POLICE CHIEF GIVES HER A
BED IN AN OFFICE

She Is Held
re For
tioning

by
JEFFREY

FONTEYN FLIES TO NEW YORK

Release after Envoy's Intervention

SUSPECT IN "PLOT" SAYS PANAMA

MARGOT FONTEYN, the ballerina,
ived in New York by air last night after
ed to leave Panama. She was released
ma City gaol before dawn and taken to
armed police.

ame Margot said she was departing at her
Panamanian Embassy in London said the
ked to leave. Referring to her imprison-
the Embassy said:
as temporarily held by the authorities
ama because she was suspected of a plot
band, Dr. Roberto Arias, to overthrow the
legally-constituted

Life In Jail For The Ballerina . . . She Enchants Her Guards, Gets A Room Of Her Own, Is Asked To Dance And Then . . . Freedom

MARGOT FLIES OUT

The Scene In The Cell—By JOHN GOLD

The Figure in White

PANAMA CITY,
Wednesday.

I SPOKE to-day to the two
men who visited Dame
where she spent 24 hours in

'Expelled? No, I Want to Leave'

From JOHN GOLD
PANAMA CITY, Wednesday:

1 am: Arias takes refuge

'EXTRADITE

PRESIDENT de la
Guardia is
weighing the possibi-
lity of lodging extra-
dition proceedings
against Dame Margot
Fonteyn — now in
Panama City
jail.

MARGOT: I TOOK NO PART IN PLOT

in the Brazilian Embassy

187

A boatload of arms being shipped to safety for the next plot had been sunk off the coast only 40 miles from Panama City.

Fishing was abandoned for more serious game.

When the Nola arrived at the wreck, the shrimp boat Elaine was already at work salvaging the arms, the crew supplemented by 11 eager young students.

Sharks

Under the eyes of Dame Margot and in the midst of a swirling school of hungry sharks, the job was completed.

Together the Nola and the Elaine set out to sea and the shelter of the sprawling Perlas Islands.

But next day they were spotted. And the fateful decision was taken which was to send Dame Margot back

School de Ba

Vive Fonteyn! Le Ballet Militant!

"Now altogether, children: 'Dame Margot, John Wayne, Errol Flynn, Merle Oberon, young Uncle Bob Arias and all . . .'"

"Now let's have the pas de deux WITHOUT the revolutionary movement."

"She's so divine in Swan Lake, of course, that imagination boggles at what her performance must be like in the Panama Canal."

NICOLAS BENTLEY

BENTLEY

"CARAMBA! THEY'RE DANCING!"

Looks more like a pas seul than a revolutionary movement to me, capitano...'

Margot talks of danger

Continued from Page 1

" What is the danger to your husband's life ? " She answered with one word : " Guns."

Only occasionally did a frown shadow her face. " I'll talk about anything," she smiled. " But, no, no, no, nothing about Panama." She said, " I wasn't active in any plot."

Someone said that Dame Margot had been likened to a " decoy duck " and a gun-toting revolutionary. She laughed and said : " I don't think I look like a duck—or like a wolf in sheep's clothing."

" Let's have the English first," Dame Margot said as a torrent of questions poured from a French newscaster. Reporters who could not jam themselves into the room threw questions from outside.

Cameras flashed and whirred. TV men shouted " Get out of the view." After 20 minutes of non-stop questioning an official asked : " Would you like to go now, Dame Margot ? "

" Not if there's anything else I can clear up," she smiled. " I want these boys to know that there will be nothing else after this. No more stories, no exclusives. I want to rest."

For ten more minutes American, European, and British correspondents tried to wrest from Dame Margot the story of herself, of the " revolution," and " what it was like in that bug-ridden jail."

Sweetly she smiled : " I was not active in any plot. Do I look as if I carry a gun ? "

Asked about her visit to Cuba and the allegation that she had been in contact with the revolutionaries there Dame Margot said she had been in Cuba last January shortly after the revolution there.

Although she had nothing to do with it she had spoken on the telephone to someone in the London Press.

" A story appeared in the London papers which was grossly exaggerated and elaborated upon and quoted me as saying things which were quite fantastic," she said.

" I am afraid it is a case of 'once bitten twice shy' I was really upset. It was stated that I was warning the British Government.

" That was a wild statement. I am a British subject and I would not be so impertinent as to tell the British Government what to do."

JEFFREY BLYTH cables from New York, Friday.—Dr. Miro, 47-year-old exiled Panamanian lawyer who declared he is going to lead an invasion of Panama early next month, shrugged off here tonight the caustic comments Dame Margot made about him in London.

" I don't want to contradict such a nice lady," he said.

Her criticisms did not appear to bother him the slightest. " I am glad to see she is in such a fighting mood," he said. " Perhaps some of it will transfer to her husband."

ice-cool amid it all

A MAGNIFICENT
entrance. A
compliment in itself
to the woman who
steps so nonchalantly
from the comparative
brilliance of a floodlit
theatre into the harsh
glare on the stage of
international politics.

Flying east from
Panama, playing cat
and mouse with
reporters at New
York, it was Dame
Margot Fonteyn who
got calm.

Here, indeed, as
an airliner comes to a
halt at London Air-
port yesterday, the
discipline of the ballet

Plots Spin, Nations Argue Over the Dancing Dame

By WALTER O'HEARN

"DAME MARGOT FONTEYN's adventures in Panama are enough, as they say, to chill the imagination. Well, not everybody's imagination. Since Mr. Oppenheim's day the thriller-writers have been stringing together such episodes, never dreaming that Dame Margot and history would catch up with them. Life imitates art, to quote Oscar Wilde.

You have been kept well informed of the Dame's adventures, but it will do no harm to skip over the highlights, just once again lightly. The former Margot Hookham, who has been described by some prose-poet as "the prima-est of British ballerinas" was married in 1955 to Dr. Roberto Arias, later Panamanian ambassador to the Court of St. James. The following year, having kept her British citizenship, she was invested as a Dame Commander of the Most Excellent Order of the British Empire. Last month she and her husband visited Panama. Dr. Arias was no longer an ambassador. Indeed he was on the outs with the government of Panama, which promptly accused him of revolutionary activity. (Accusations are flying pretty thick in Panama these days. John Wayne, the film actor, was also accused by somebody of being involved in the plot. Wayne said he was shocked.)

Last weekend Dr. Arias and wife were cruising the Gulf of Panama aboard the chartered yacht Nola. According to the government of President Ernesto de la Guardia, the ex-ambassador was really engaged in a plot of "vast ramifications" and the purpose of his little cruise was to seize the garrison at Santa Clara. Thereupon, Dr. Arias—wise man—went underground, or at least ashore, while Dame Margot and a boatman sailed serenely into Balboa.

(The image of the lone ballerina sailing serenely into Balboa is pretty special. Oppenheim never conjured up anything like it. Graham Greene, Eric Ambler and Manning Coles had better hide their heads.)

The lady was arrested at once, but in a very classy way. She was taken to the Panama City jail, to the special quarters on the top floor which are known for certain historical reasons as "the presidential suite". Rumor has it that Dame Margot was given a hi-fi set in case she wanted to dance. Obviously, in Panamanian protocol, there's nothing like a Dame.

Almost at once the wheels of Her Majesty's Government of the United Kingdom, still the most efficient of diplomatic engines, began to turn. British Ambassador Sir Ian Henderson was at the Panama Foreign Office with a protest as fast as his Humber saloon could carry him. After two nights and a day in the presidential suite Dame Margot was released with apologies and whisked aboard a plane bound for New York. As John Profumo, Minister of State for Foreign Affairs, told the House of Commons it was a "regrettable incident".

Regrettable perhaps. But those of us who have sighed and wished that life would catch up with a story book world won't regret it entirely. We wouldn't want to see a hair of Dame Margot's head touched, naturally, or even a hair of Roberto Arias's head. But the dancer is safe, the Marlon Brando divorce was almost crowded out of the news, the Dalai Lama has a glamorous competitor, and life for once has gaiety and a warm sort of absurdity. Dame Margot Fonteyn is reported to have a "bubbly sense of humor". My source is the New York Times, which is sparing of adjectives like bubbly. This in my book acquits her of any part in any revolution.

Now how did Fidel Castro get in this act? Because, as usual, a reporter put him there. Dame Margot arrived at Idlewild Airport Thursday, while Fidel Castro was delighting and astounding New York, and a reporter at the airport, referring to the rumor that Dr. Arias was in league with Fidel Castro, asked the dancer did she intend to visit Premier Castro.

"No, I don't think I shall," the Dame replied.

She wasn't going to meet Galina Ulanova, either. But we already have too many larger-than-Oppenheim characters in this script. Let's leave it there and rejoice in truth's triumph over fiction."

With Sir Winston and Lady Churchill, touring Venice from the Onassis yacht Christina, July 1960

Margot will be ballet 'guest'

DAME MARGOT FONTEYN, prima ballerina of the Royal Opera House, Covent Garden, will in future appear only as a "guest" of the Royal Ballet.

There has been no divorce or row between Dame Margot and the Royal.

Nor, said Mr. David L. Webster, general administrator of the opera house, is there any truth in a suggestion that Dame Margot has refused to sign a contract.

He said that last night's "guest" statement simply means that her position as a world prima ballerina has been recognised by the theatre where she first won fame.

In demand

"In recent years Dame Margot has been more and more in demand for performances all over the world, a right and fitting tribute to her supreme position," he added.

"It is also right that her time should be completely at her own disposal and not subject to the demands and policy of the Royal Ballet.

"This arrangement has been made at the suggestion of the company and with the agreement of Dame Margot. She will be with us again in the August season.

"Talk of a contract refused is ridiculous. I don't believe I've proffered a piece of paper to Dame Margot for years. All our arrangements have been verbal."

Flying back

Dame Margot left Rio de Janeiro last night by air for London. She went to Brazil to join her husband, Dr. Roberto Arias, who was flown there from Panama, where he led an abortive revolt. She will return there to join him later this month.

Dame Margot said that when she is in London she will discuss with her partner, Michael Somes, an invitation to dance in Brazil. She hoped he would return with her.

In Warsaw she appears with the Polish National Ballet in *Swan Lake*, partnered by Michael Somes. Speaking from the stage afterwards, the head of the Warsaw Ballet School says "Tonight I have seen again the greatest dancer of the age."

On 10th July Margot reads in a morning paper that she has been made Guest Artist with The Royal Ballet. This follows a protest from her that the administration had raised the prices of seats for her performances, a practice normally reserved for guest artists who appear in limited seasons only. She continues however to dance frequently with The Royal Ballet.

On 24th December 1959, Margot travels to Monte Carlo, and on 29th December appears as The Firebird in a Gala at the Monte Carlo Opera House to celebrate the 50th anniversary of the formation of the Diaghilev Ballet. Later in the week she is seen in the *Casse-Noisette pas de deux*, and *Seène d'Amour*.

In London, at a "Midnight Matinée" in aid of victims of the Fréjus flood disaster, Margot dances an extract from *Birthday Offering*.

In January 1960, Fonteyn dances the *Sylvia pas de deux* in Brussels; Milan sees her in *La Péri* in February. March is ushered in with a Benevolent Gala at Covent Garden, where *Scène d'Amour* has a single performance at the Opera House. April finds Fonteyn at a State Gala at Covent Garden honouring the President of the French Republic, General de Gaulle, who sees her dance the *grand pas de deux* from Act III of *The Sleeping Beauty*. In May she is in Finland and Belgium; in June, South America — appearing with the Ballet de Rio. With Somes she appears in *La Péri* and the *Sylvia pas de deux*. July is a holiday month; Dr. and Mrs. Arias take a Mediterranean cruise as guests of Mr. Aristotle Onassis. Fellow guests are Sir Winston and Lady Churchill. At the Edinburgh Festival in August, La Fonteyn appears as La Péri.

Ashton devises a pas de deux, Rêve d'Amour, from Glazunov's Raymonda, for a Gala on 26th November 1959, in aid of the Royal Academy of Dancing. Danced by Fonteyn and Somes, the work is later retitled Scène d'Amour

In the Summer of 1960, Tamara Karsavina supervises the revised production of Giselle, first seen on the American Tour in September. Many of the traditional mime passages are restored to the ballet

Greeting H. R. H. Princess Margaret, President of The Royal Ballet, at a première of a film in which Fonteyn appears in The Firebird, Ondine and Swan Lake Act II

On 6th September she leaves for America, to join The Royal Ballet on its Sixth Tour of the United States, scheduled to last five months.

In a car following the ambassadorial coach to the Palace

1st December, with her husband, safely restored to political favour (and to London), Margot returns from the American Tour to supervise another Gala for the R.A.D. The Benefit takes place on 8th December, and Margot dances her Firebird rôle

On 13th December Dr. Arias presents his credentials for a further term as Panamanian Ambassador to the Court of St. James.

On 19th December, Margot flies to Chicago to rejoin The Royal Ballet's North American Tour.

In April 1961, Fonteyn's second visit to Japan takes place. The Royal Ballet appears in Tokyo and Osaka; and also in Hong Kong and Manila.

In June she leaves with the Company on its visit to Russia, where she dances in Leningrad and Moscow

Russia 1961

With Alla Shelest in Leningrad

With Galina Ulanova in Moscow

Before performing The Sleeping Beauty *in Leningrad*

The Sleeping Beauty, Act I, on the stage of the Kirov Theatre (formerly the Maryinsky), where the ballet was originally premièred in January 1890

Act III pas de deux with Michael Somes, Leningrad

Leaving Leningrad

Karsavina rehearses Fonteyn in Le Spectre de la Rose, 1961

The Russian influence in Fonteyn's balletic training continues spasmodically throughout her career; first with Gontcharov, then Astafieva and Preobrajenska in particular, and in specific rôles coaching from Madame Karsavina herself.

At the Royal Ballet School, with Lord Soulbury, left, admiring de Glehn's portrait of Karsavina as Columbine; after officially opening the school's premises at White Lodge, Richmond, 31st July 1957

Below left, with Cocteau's Karsavina poster for the original production of Spectre

Rehearsed by Karsavina

ZOE DOMINIC

COLL. DANCING TIMES

Fonteyn's portrait of Chloë continues as one of her most captivating performances. David Blair appears as Daphnis during this period

Performing at the Temple of Bacchus, Baalbek, in Act II (left) and Act III (above) of Swan Lake, with David Blair as Siegfried and Bryan Ashbridge as Benno

The Royal Ballet Tour of Baalbek, Damascus and Athens, August 1961

In October she invites the young Russian dancer Rudolf Nureyev, recently 'jumped' to the West, to appear in her R.A.D. Charity Gala. Sir Frederick Ashton agrees to devise a solo for Nureyev's first appearance in England.

On 2nd November, at the Gala, she appears in *Le Spectre de la Rose* (opposite) partnered by John Gilpin, as well as the *Birthday Offering pas de deux* with Michael Somes.

Left, at her home, greeting Nureyev

Below, with William Chappell looking at costume designs, while Nureyev checks the musical score with Ashton

Rehearsing Le Spectre de la Rose with Gilpin

Left, with Somes in the wings, watching Nureyev in Ashton's Poème Tragique. Somes' appearance with Fonteyn, in the pas de deux from Birthday Offering, marks their last performance together in strictly classical rôles. Neither dancer can foresee the crowded decade lying just ahead

Rehearsing Giselle with Nureyev, at Covent Garden

Beauty and the Beast, with David Blair

On 25th December 1961, with The Royal Ballet, she dances a Christmas matinée performance of *The Sleeping Beauty* in Monte Carlo. It is there, on 29th December, that she appears in John Cranko's *Beauty and the Beast,* for the Société des Bains de Mer.

She also has agreed to dance with the young Tartar, Nureyev, in three performances of *Giselle*; the tickets are over-subscribed by 70,000 applications.

On 21st February 1962, the first Fonteyn/Nureyev *Giselle* causes a sensation. Nureyev joins The Royal Ballet as permanent Guest Artist along with Fonteyn.

On 26th March 1962 she leaves for
a tour of Australia and New Zealand
with The Touring Section of The
Royal Ballet Company.
Her repertoire includes:
  Swan Lake Act II
  Le Spectre de la Rose
  Beauty and the Beast
  Sylvia pas de deux
  Birthday Offering
  Scène d'Amour
  Symphonic Variations
  Aurora's Wedding
  L'Entrée de Madame Butterfly

In June 1962, at the Bath Festival she
appears in *Swan Lake* Act II with
David Blair; Yehudi Menuhin plays
the violin solo. At the end of the
London Season she takes 26 curtain
calls at Covent Garden.

COLL. AMBROSE

At the Nervi Festival, in an open air performance by The Royal Ballet, she appears with Nureyev in Swan Lake – their first together

During June she appears on television in a version of Giselle Act II pas de deux with Nureyev, above

Left, before a camera rehearsal

MIKE DAVIS

Le Corsaire
pas de deux

She learns the Russian *pas de deux Le Corsaire* from Nureyev, and appears with him when the *pas de deux* is premièred at a Gala on 3rd November. The applause lasts longer than the ballet itself.

DAILY EXPRESS

Rehearsing Gayaneh with Viktor Rona, in front of the current Drury Lane set

Gayaneh
pas de deux

Following the huge success of the *Corsaire pas de deux*, she follows it a few days later with another imported *pas de deux*, *Gayaneh*, this time with the Hungarian dancer Viktor Rona.

The delightful Kurdish-style dance is one of the hits at her R.A.D. Benevolent Fund Gala.

She repeats it (again with Viktor Rona) during a guest appearance in Washington with the American Ballet Theatre at a Kennedy Gala on 12th December 1962. She has already lunched with President Kennedy the day before.

with Viktor Rona

215

Because of an injury to Nureyev's foot, the ballet which Ashton has been devising for Fonteyn and Nureyev has to be postponed. On 7th February 1963, Nureyev appears again at Covent Garden, this time in *Swan Lake* (as *Le Lac des Cygnes* has now come to be billed). The Russian dances Siegfried to Fonteyn's Odette/Odile. Traditionalists criticise certain changed passages, but Fonteyn is considered to have given yet another "performance of a lifetime" and the ballet itself is patently ready for much rethinking in the form of a new production. Nureyev has been doubtful of Fonteyn's wisdom in dancing *Swan Lake* with him. At first he comments: "It is too dangerous – I will destroy you," meaning that her cool lyricism and line will be unbalanced, and suffer in contrast with his more tempestuous manner and baroque style.

In the event, she accepts the challenge. Nureyev is heard to concede later: "It is your best rôle – and you *are* the best."

Left,
Swan Lake

Right,
Symphonic
Variations

At this time she continues to appear in another of the key rôles in her career – in Symphonic Variations. Left, rehearsing the ballet with Nureyev

Rehearsals for the new Ashton ballet finally continue in a fever of advance publicity. The work is on the theme of Dumas' perennial *La Dame aux Camélias*. The designer for the ballet is Cecil Beaton (below), while the music is to be, naturally, Liszt.

Ashton's new ballet, called *Marguerite and Armand,* is premièred on 12th March 1963 at a Royal Ballet Benevolent Fund Gala.

Marguerite
and
Armand

With Leslie Edwards as Marguerit's Ducal protector

With Rudolf Nureyev as Armand

Armand's father asks that Marguerite give up the liaison with his son – for the sake of the younger man's future.

With Michael Somes as Armand's father

Marguerite and Armand

220

The ballet is destined to provide an enduring showcase for Fonteyn's dramatic talents.

In July 1971, Peter Williams is to write in *Dance and Dancers* "…her performances this year must surely amount to the great theatrical wonder of our time."

– on Fonteyn as Marguerite

In April 1963 she is asked again about the question of retirement and she replies, again "I just go on and on." She has already been quoted as saying "I see no end to my dancing."

On 17th April the 7th North American Tour takes place.
"The Fonteyn – Nureyev Black Swan *pas de deux* stopped the performance for a full five minutes of cheering. During the virtuoso passage, after all of the shouting for Nureyev, she sensationally topped him in an *attitude en arabesque* that she held and held and held, evoking the loudest screams of all. As well as complementing each other superbly, Fonteyn and Nureyev also demand the utmost from each other in every phase of a performance."
P.W. Manchester
after *Swan Lake* in New York

Margot first dances extracts from the Bournonville version of *La Sylphide* in Athens in July, during a "Fonteyn's Follies" concert tour, in which her repertoire includes *Le Corsaire, Gayaneh, La Sylphide pas de deux* and the Grand Pas Hongroise from *Raymonda* – all danced with Nureyev; as well as *Birthday Offering* and *Symphonic Variations* with Royes Fernandez, and *Scène d'Amour* with Ronald Hynd.

La Sylphide

Rehearsing with Royes Fernandez in the Herod Atticus Theatre, Athens

The Fonteyn Concert Tour includes
    Athens,
    Nice,
    Tel Aviv,
    Haifa,
    Jerusalem,
    Nagoya,
    Kyoto,
    Osaka,
    Honolulu

Backstage in Kyoto – wearing her current Raymonda costume

In the Autumn she appears with The Royal Ballet in Paris at the First International Ballet Festival.

With Nureyev as James, The Highlander who causes unwittingly the death of the Sylphide

223

La Bayadère

27th November sees the Covent Garden première of *La Bayadère* Act IV; the famous 'white act' of the Petipa ballet reproduced by Rudolf Nureyev for The Royal Ballet. Fonteyn appears as the spirit of Nikiya the temple dancer, sought in the Kingdom of the Shades by the warrior Solor, danced by Nureyev.

"We expected Nureyev to shine… but it was Fonteyn who dazzled even more. This was Fonteyn the superlative stylist, and also Fonteyn the amazing technician, dancing with extraordinary speed and superb assurance. She contrived to make dramatic sense of the characterisation, but most importantly, she showed an absolute authority in dealing with the choreographic manner which is pre-eminently virtuosic."

Clement Crisp, *Financial Times*

"Ballet may have previously known a career that followed the curious path of Margot Fonteyn's, but if it has I cannot recall hearing of it. The old idea of dancing being a young person's art is certainly not true. No dancer reaches their prime until they are over 30, and their years at the peak – the better the dancer the more true this is – are much longer than popular legend would have us accept. But the almost unbelievable thing about Fonteyn is quite simply that she has kept on improving some distance past the age when improvement would normally be thought out of the question. Nor by improvement do I mean merely the increasing artistry which any great ballerina certainly acquires over the years. This enrichment is, of course, true of Fonteyn, but in her unique case the improvement has also been technical – partially this is a matter of physique, for she still has the figure of a young girl, and in fact her physique is probably better now than ever before."

"*Bayadère* provided what was virtually a quantitative check on Fonteyn's physical prowess. For here she was dancing a bravura rôle with considerable distinction, in a way that would, I think, have been beyond her fifteen, ten, five or even two years ago."

"Of course, Fonteyn's balances have for many years been outstanding, and *Bayadère* exploited them. But the ballet also exploited a whole technical armoury that one hardly knew she possessed. Her turns, both supported and unsupported have never been stronger or faster, and surely she has never jumped so high or danced so effortlessly. The placing of her body looked glorious. Here she was contrasted with three very strong young dancers – any of the six probably rather stronger than Fonteyn was at their age. But Fonteyn's authority over them was never for one instant in doubt."

Clive Barnes, *Dance and Dancers*

"Fonteyn, as no one else, is so lightly posed in her arabesques, that it seems her toe caresses the ground."

Tamara Karsavina

with Rudolf Nureyev

The La Sylphide pas de deux is rehearsed (a little unconventionally) for the R.A.D. Charity Gala on 5th December

With Blair at the dress rehearsal of Swan Lake

In December 1963 Nureyev is injured in a street accident, and David Blair steps in to partner Fonteyn in the new production of *Swan Lake*, which includes a Prologue with Odette seen as the Princess before her transformation to a swan.

The first performance of the new production takes place on 12th December.

"I was amazed at the powerful impression her performance made on me. I simply wept in the course of the last act, and that's an odd thing to happen to a professional dancer who has seen *Swan Lake* hundreds of times and danced in it herself. But that's the effect Margot Fonteyn's artistry had on me."

Natalia Makarova

In Ashton's new Prologue to Swan Lake

The New Year of 1964 finds Margot endowed with the Freedom of the City of Rio de Janeiro. During January she makes appearances with the San Francisco Ballet Co., in California, as well as St. Louis, Chicago and Mexico City.

In February she returns to *Ondine* at Covent Garden, partnered by Donald MacLeary.

From 27th–30th May she guests at Stuttgart, partnered by Nureyev in *Swan Lake,* and also in *La Sylphide pas de deux* and *Le Corsaire pas de deux.*

Above, leaving London Airport with Nureyev 10th April, for Australia, to appear with the Australian Ballet Company

With her husband after the performance

Arriving in Melbourne

Left, signing autographs for ballerinas of the Kirov, Natalia Makarova and Irina Kolpakhova

There was a Dame Margot Fonteyn
Who scarcely had time to complain
That the worst choreography
In the whole Physiography
Was the steps into each aeroplane

Montevideo 1957

London, from New York 1954

Japan, to New Zealand 1959

London, from Australia 1964

Australia, from London 1970

London, to New York 1963

Left, Tokyo 1961

24th May, with her mother, after arriving back at London Airport

Mid-day, 9th June

On 8th June 1964 while in the city of Bath to rehearse for Yehudi Menuhin's Bath Festival of the Arts, she learns late at night that her husband has been wounded in a shooting incident in Panama. His spokesmen advise her to complete the first performance for the Festival the following day, before leaving for Panama. During the day she rehearses, then performs the *La Sylphide pas de deux* in the opening performance, as well as premièring the new work devised by Kenneth MacMillan, *Divertimento,* with Menuhin playing Bartok's solo violin piece.

On 9th June, after *Divertimento* (below), the audience demands an encore of the entire work.

That night she leaves for London Airport with her stepson Roberto jr., en route for Panama.

Divertimento

with Rudolf Nureyev

(MII2) PANAMA CITY, JUNE 11-(AP)--British ballerina
Dame Margot Fonteyn is escorted by Dr. Harmodio Arias
Jr., left, a brother-in-law, and U.S. businessman
Robert McGrath after she arrived at the Panama air-
port last night en route to bedside of her husband,
Dr. Roberto Arias Jr. who was shot Monday by a
political associate. At top right is her stepson,
Roberto Arias, who arrived with her. (AP Wirephoto)

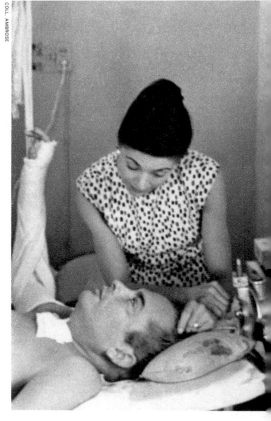

Alarmed by the true nature of her husband's injuries she remains in Panama, and Lynn Seymour
deputises for her in *La Sylphide* at the second of her scheduled appearances at the Bath Festival. Her
forthcoming appearance with The Royal Ballet in *The Sleeping Beauty* is cancelled.

(MH3)PANAMA CITY, JUNE 12--(AP)---After visiting her wounded husband, Dr. Roberto Arias, in a hospital here, Dame Marget Fonteyn, with her arm around her stepson, Roberto Arias, Jr., walks along a corridor with Dr. Octavio Vallarino, left, one of the surgeons attending Arias. Arias was shot three times last Sunday by a disgruntled political associate. (AP Wirephoto)(jsb1915GMT)1964.

Returning to London Airport for performances with The Royal Ballet, temporarily housed at the Theatre Royal, Drury Lane

Dr. Arias is flown specially to England for treatment at the famous spinal injuries centre at Stoke Mandeville

During the Summer she has been rehearsing with The Royal Ballet's Touring Section in Rudolf Nureyev's reproduction of the full-length Petipa *Raymonda*, planned for a première at the Festival of The Two Worlds in Spoleto, Italy. She arrives in Spoleto for the opening, but is called back to her husband's bedside in England. He survives a crisis, and later she flies back to Spoleto.

Margot first dances as Raymonda at the final performance in Spoleto. There are 32 curtain calls at the end of the performance.

The Royal Ballet Tour continues to Lebanon to appear at the Baalbek Festival. There Margot repeats her huge success in her newest Petipa heroine rôle, that of Raymonda the Hungarian princess, as well as making a notable return to the rôle of Ophelia in *Hamlet,* after a gap of twenty years.

Raymonda in Spoleto

She also dances in Act III of *The Sleeping Beauty* (above) in which Nureyev reinstates a version of the old Petipa coda for the Prince and Aurora. A certain powerful critic, noticing this new interpolation, writes later: "If Dame Margot thinks she is a better choreographer than Petipa, I have to tell her she is not."

In Vienna, in the Autumn, Nureyev is busy supervising every aspect of his new production of *Swan Lake* which is to be premièred with himself and Fonteyn at the Vienna State Opera in October.

Trying costumes for Nureyev's production of Swan Lake in Vienna

Ophelia in Baalbek, Lebanon, 1964

On 15th October the new Swan Lake is acclaimed by the Viennese audience

By November, Fonteyn is in the thick of the London Season with The Royal Ballet. Austria, meanwhile, has printed a special stamp to commemorate the recent performances.

During her time at Stoke Mandeville, Margot has driving tuition and passes a driving test at her first attempt. This enables her to drive herself to and from the Stoke Mandeville railway station, from which point she commutes to London for classes.

Paquita

Prior to 17th November Margot is busy organising yet another Charity Gala for the financially precarious Royal Academy of Dancing. At the same time she learns *Paquita* from Nureyev, for part of the programme.

With Nureyev in Paquita, 17th November

29th November. For a special television tribute to Sir Winston Churchill on his 90th birthday, Fonteyn is persuaded (in a choice much against her will) to dance Fokine's *The Dying Swan,* so particularly associated with Pavlova in Churchill's younger theatre-going days.

SEQUENCE ANTHONY CRICKMAY

The Dying Swan

During November she appears again in Daphnis and Chloë, this time with Christopher Gable as Daphnis

In Washington, where she appears in the Corsaire pas de deux with Nureyev during the Inaugural Gala for President Johnson on 18th January 1965

Throughout January, Kenneth MacMillan is rehearsing his first full-length work, *Romeo and Juliet*. This ballet is made, essentially, for other dancers, but Fonteyn and Nureyev are announced as the principal pair for the first night.

The week before the new ballet's opening is full of problems. Nureyev's ankle is giving trouble, and on 5th February his rôle opposite Fonteyn in *La Bayadère* is taken by Christopher Gable, at the shortest notice – three minutes before the curtain rises.

9th February 1965; Fonteyn essays the rôle of Juliet, with Nureyev as Romeo, at the première of *Romeo and Juliet*. Afterwards there are 43 curtain calls for the ballet and its dancers.

Romeo and Juliet

MIKE DAVIS

Juliet

At Stoke Mandeville, talking to a patient in the canteen; and with her husband during the many months of Dr. Arias' gradual rehabilitation

Above, 29th September 1964 and, right, 16th February 1965

On 23rd March 1965 she is presented with a golden replica of the new rose "Margot Fonteyn"

The long months of commuting drag on. After any evening performance there is a frantic rush to the station to catch the last train.

In April there is a rehearsal for a Covent Garden Gala, at which Fonteyn, in *Birthday Offering*, injures a leg while making a jump. She gets through the actual performance (with restrictions) but is forced to cancel the much anticipated *Sleeping Beauty* due for the 10th April. She does, however, make her scheduled appearances with the Company in New York at the beginning of its 8th North American Tour. It is during this season that Olga Spessivtseva is seen in public for the first time in many years – having been escorted by Anton Dolin to see *Giselle* again.

From New York, Margot comes back to London, enabling her to be with her husband, and allowing her to appear at Covent Garden with the other section of The Royal Ballet, before returning for the remainder of the American Tour.

On 2nd June 1965, at Covent Garden, she is partnered by Attilio Labis (guest artist from the Paris Opéra) in *Swan Lake*, and also in one final appearance in the full-length *Sylvia*.

The *Swan Lakes* are considered a particular triumph, as is "...Dame Margot Fonteyn's wonderful portrayal of Sylvia, better, more exultant than ever after an absence of many years... a lambent radiance..."

The Times

In October she appears with The Royal Ballet in Milan, Rome, Naples and Bologna.

With Attilio Labis in Act III of Sylvia

Sylvia in her pizzicato solo, June 1965

Fonteyn and Nureyev appear as guest artists in another production of Nureyev's full-length staging of *Raymonda* during The Australian Ballet Company's English Tour. The production is premièred in Birmingham on 6th November 1965.

"This rôle exposes mercilessly any weakness in the ballerina who attempts it. On the other hand, it shows off to perfection the virtues of the ballerina worthy of it. Fonteyn assumes it with daring, wears it with grace, and warms it with majesty . . . Her performance is a whole: you see it as complete in itself, clearly bounded, sharply outlined, and stretching also to the full limits of its right scope. It has harmony: within itself, in its balance and rhythm, its variety and continuity, in line and colour; and harmony also with what is about it, with the music, her partner, the other dancers, the sense of the drama. And then it has radiance, a quality of light and warmth that shines from within, a divine spark illuminating the mortal achievement."

John Percival
Dance and Dancers

Raymonda

At the first performance of *Cinderella,* on 23rd December 1948, Fonteyn had been prevented by injury from appearing. On 23rd December 1965, exactly seventeen years later, no such misfortune prevents her from making an enchanting appearance as the heroine, on the opening night of the new production of *Cinderella.* With her are Ashton, Helpmann, Grant and Edwards in their original rôles.

"Margot Fonteyn's Cinderella is incomparable. Even faced with cohorts of young and pretty dancers as we were last night, she struck me as the most beautiful. Her every gesture, the slightest muscular movement is a joy or tear which we share and an integral part of being Cinderella – to such an extent that even seeing her stand still is moving. And few dancers ever learn that."

Susan Lester

"So far, amazingly after 17 years, she remains without an equal in the part."

Peter Williams

With Robert Helpmann and Frederick Ashton as the Ugly Sisters

Cinderella

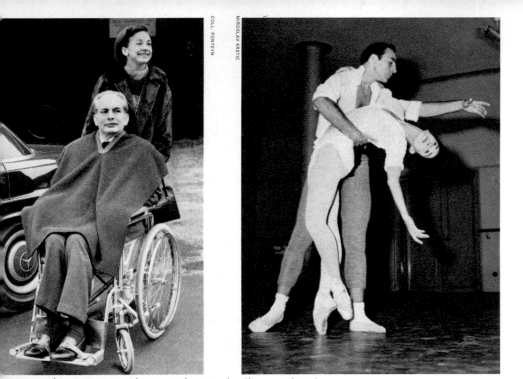

During April 1966 she guests (with Keith Rosson) in the Festival Ballet's two-ballerina version of *Swan Lake*, appearing (as Odette) in Barcelona, Madrid, Lisbon, Bilbao and Palma.

During the year she also films the Vienna *Swan Lake* with Nureyev. Then follows a European Tour by The Royal Ballet.
May: Germany, Finland, Norway, Belgium, Holland.
June: Monte Carlo, Athens, Florence.

Luxembourg – Prague – Brno – Bratislava – Belgrade – Sofia – Warsaw....

During September and October, on the Eastern European Tour with The Royal Ballet, Fonteyn appears in *The Firebird* again, as well as *Swan Lake* (with MacLeary), *Daphnis and Chloë* (with Gable) and *Scène d'Amour* (with Hynd).

Above, Dr. Arias leaves Stoke Mandeville on 12th February
Right, rehearsing Scène d'Amour with Ronald Hynd in Belgrade
Below, photographed during a break in Ondine rehearsals at the Studios of the B.B.C.

"Last night Fonteyn danced *Swan Lake;* superlatives will not do, analysis is impossible; what can one say that will do justice – if not honour – to such an interpretation? It needs the pen of Valéry, Levinson, Edwin Denby, to capture something of its greatness. I must content myself with recording that it was magnificent on all counts, faultless in style, immensely touching in its tragedy and poetry....

Fonteyn imbues Odette with immense pathos; the tragedy assumes heroic stature, we are compelled into a belief in the work as a dramatic experience rather than as the usual handsome display of lyrical dancing. For once the sorrowing duet of violin and 'cello in the *pas de deux* is exactly matched in the emotional shaping of the movement, and the whole technical machinery of the work – music, doomed lovers, choreographic outline – finds its perfect expression in the figures of Odette and Siegfried. Fonteyn, amazingly, has succeeded in suggesting an even greater force in Odette's agonised hopelessness, and the separation at the end of the scene is extraordinary in its despair.

I have always thought Fonteyn's Odile the most beguiling of enchantresses, and the most malevolent; last night there were terrifying flashes of evil – a baleful glance flashed suddenly at the ecstatic Siegfried as Odile moved away from him was chillingly effective. As a display of bravura dancing the *pas de deux* was entirely thrilling. Fonteyn's authority and her classic restraint even in the most arduous, culminated in a scintillating coda. As in the Lake scenes the choreography was beautifully shaped, perfectly phrased, totally meaningful."

Clement Crisp
The Financial Times 8. 2. 66

Right, with David Wall after their first Swan Lake together

With Labis, she rehearses a scene from Ondine for performance on British television

Following the excerpt of *Ondine* on T.V., Fonteyn appears with Labis in the full-length *Ondine* at Covent Garden in November and December.

She also dances *Cinderella* with Donald MacLeary; and *Swan Lake*, on tour, with David Wall; also *The Sleeping Beauty, Swan Lake* and *Giselle* with Nureyev, back at Covent Garden.

On 23rd February 1967 Roland Petit's *Paradise Lost* is first seen at a Covent Garden Gala. Fonteyn and Nureyev cope most successfully with a new idiom and much Op-Art distraction around them.

In May, after rehearsals in London, she flies to Kansas for the performances of a new ballet-masque choreographed by Marina Svetlova. Fonteyn plays the part of Elizabeth I of England, and Attilio Labis plays Essex. The production is part of the Purcell Festival. On 27th May *The Fairie Queene (Elizabeth and Essex)* opens in Kansas.

Left, with Donald MacLeary in Cinderella

The Fairie Queene

As Queen Elizabeth I of England

With Attilio Labis as Essex

Paradise Lost

As Eve, with Rudolf Nureyev as Adam

enjoy in Hippieland."

She added: "Miss Fonteyn threw us when she asked for tea — that's slang for marijuana, you know. But I knew she really wanted a cup of tea and I got her one.

...as the kind of affair we

NO ARREST 'IF FONTEYN HAD NOT PANICKED'

ATTORNEY'S EXPLANATION

By MABEL ELLIOTT
SAN FRANCISCO, Wednesday

ROYAL Ballet Company officials were silent today on

Hippies plan a love-in for Fonteyn

From JEFFREY BLYTH: SAN FRANCISCO, Wednesday

EXTRA police have been detailed to guard San Francisco's opera house tonight against a "love-in" by Hippies demonstrating their affection for ballerina Dame Margot Fonteyn.

Several thousand of the long-haired teenagers whose aggression is usually limited to throwing flower petals at the police, are planning to besiege the opera house.

Dame Margot was arrested and jailed for five hours yesterday after visiting a Hippyland party.

One teenage girl said: "She may wear ermine but she is one of us now. She played it so cool."

The girl, in a rainbow-coloured mod dress hung with exotic beads and bangles, was passing out hand-lettered leaflets urging fellow Hippyland residents to attend the love-in.

Last night after they heard police had decided to drop charges several hundred Hippies gathered outside the opera house in the hope of seeing Dame Margot and her dancing partner Rudolf Nureyev. But it was their night off.

Sneaked

The Hippies danced for a while in the street—before heading back to Haight-Ashbury, the run-down neighbourhood which is the heart of Hippyland.

Dame Margot and her fellow Royal Ballet dancers were invited to Monday night's party by Paul Wesley, 26, a philosophy graduate from Trinity College, Dublin, now hitch-hiking round the world and temporarily living in Hippyland.

He and a friend, Martin Wong, sneaked backstage after the night's performance of the Royal Ballet, asked for autographs from Dame Margot and Nureyev, and then asked if they would like to visit them.

Today Dame Margot said she had found the Hippies "nice people."

Another member of the ballet said: "Rudi was very exuberant. He put on an impromptu ballet."

When the police arrived, someone shouted: "It's the fuzz—everyone buzz." The party broke up in an undignified scramble for the staircase leading to the roof.

Dame Margot, who had arrived carrying a bunch of red roses, fell over a dustbin in the dark.

A police flashlight revealed her in her white ermine coat hiding behind a parapet.

20-MINUTE APPLAUSE FOR DAME MARGOT A NUREY

best for Small Ads

No. 28,392

The Evening Star
and STAR
LONDON TUESDAY JULY 11 1967

Evening Sale

A police report tonight tells of swoop in 'Hippieland'

'MARGOT, NUREYEV IN PARTY RAID

overseas page overseas page

Margot and Rudy —the charges are dropped

San Francisco, Wednesday

Daily Telegraph
and Morning Post
Printed in LONDON and MANCHESTER. 4d.

4.30 a.m.

FONTEYN & NU
CHARGES DROP

DANCERS ARRESTED

WEDNESDAY

THE INDEPENDENT NEWSPAPER

Police escort for Dame Margot

FONTEYN CHARGE IS CALLED OFF

From JOHN SAMPSON
NEW YORK, Tuesday

DAME MARGOT FONTEYN was arrested early today as she sat on a San Francisco rooftop wearing a white ermine coat. A police officer said: "She was very graceful."

Her ballet partner, 28-year-old Rudolf Nureyev, was found lying face down on an adjoining roof.

The policeman also said: "He looked immaculate, even though he didn't have a tie."

Dame Margot and Nureyev were charged with visiting a place where marijuana is used or kept, and with disturbing the peace.

Late tonight the District Attorney's office announced that charges against the ballet stars would be dropped.

Mr. Whisman, assistant district attorney, said there was insufficient

"No complaint will be filed against any of the individuals concerned with the decision had with the identity of any involved.

After rooftop arrest with Nureyev in Hippieland

Booms nearly launch lifeboat

A TOWN'S lifeboat crew raced to action stations yesterday for the

SUN

JULY 12 1967 · FOURPENCE · No. 875

Brazil

Some More Unusual Situations

Japan

Canada

Rehearsal Time

Remembering Cinderella choreography, with David Blair, 1965

At a Bayadère rehearsal, with Fernando Bujones, 1973

…and with Nureyev and Gable, 1964

The fun…

…and the
pain of it

During the 9th North American Tour by The Royal Ballet, in the Spring and Summer of 1967, a Fonteyn performance in *Swan Lake* closes the New York season. Margot is awarded an astonishing 42½ minute ovation at the end of the ballet.

On 6th November, under a quaint newspaper headline which reads: "FONTEYN CONQUERS SWEDES" English readers learn of the great success of a performance by Fonteyn and Nureyev in *Swan Lake* in Stockholm. Black Market tickets are reported as having fetched an all-time high of over £100 per seat.

Night Shadow

With John Gilpin as The Poet

With Nureyev in Birthday Offering, 1968

With Richard Cragun in Les Sylphides, danced in York with R.A.D. students and also in the Coliseum, London, for a televised programme

Through Venice, Naples, Turin and Brescia in January 1968, she tours with the Festival Ballet Company, appearing in *The Sleeping Beauty,* and also trying once more the Balanchine idiom, this time the romantic *Night Shadow* ("La Sonnambula"), which she first dances on 1st February, in Naples.

In the Spring of 1968 she appears in the Royal Ballet's 10th New York season.

12th June; at London's New Theatre she appears as a guest artist in Festival Ballet's production of *Night Shadow* (far left). It is 23 years since her last appearance in the same theatre.

1968. The year sees a pattern of constant touring for Fonteyn. After her guest appearances with Festival Ballet, and The Royal Ballet's New York season in the Spring, there are visits by The Royal Ballet Touring Section to Holland, Switzerland, Germany, France, Monaco, Italy, Spain and Portugal.

There are performances in London and the provinces, as well as filming in London, Venice, Panama, New York and Paris. On 24th October Fonteyn and Nureyev arrive in Iran. Both dancers are to appear in special performances to honour the Shah's birthday.

Above, in Venice, filming scenes for a documentary on her life and work

Left, in Panama, with her husband once more on a political campaign

Leaving Euston Station for performances
in the North of England

At a press reception, with a difficult 'guest'

"Dame Margot has achieved the almost impossible dream of any dancer: to acquire full artistic and emotional maturity while remaining in total command of her physical instrument, her body... Dame Margot has grown with time, yet not diminished.

Today, Dame Margot's Juliet is one of her most refined, most perfect portrayals, untouched and vulnerable, yet sweeping into love with the unthinking passion of nature. It is the heroic coloring of her innocence that is so affecting, and when she gives herself to love the giving is so total, so abandoned, the very cold injustice of her destiny is enough to make stones bleed and the stars cry."

Clive Barnes, on *Romeo and Juliet*
The New York Times 24. 4. 68

269

"There are times when Margot Fonteyn is not just the world's ballet superstar, but much more simply the very heartbeat of what is, after all, still her company.

When The Royal Ballet ended its six weeks' stint at the Metropolitan Opera House last night, Dame Margot danced in *The Sleeping Beauty*. She got more cheers and plaudits on entry than most ballerinas get on exit, and from then on the audience was hers and she was the audience's. She has been dancing Aurora for 30 years – before most of the present company was born. Yet she has never been better."

Clive Barnes
The New York Times 2. 6. 69

Left and below, Raymonda Act III, photographed in St. Louis, with Rudolf Nureyev as Jean de Brienne

After a subfusc première of a new Petit ballet at Covent Garden, The Royal Ballet begins its 11th visit to America on 22nd April 1969. The tour includes Canada, and is to last until 27th July.

"Perhaps Merlin, who was English stands behind Dame Margot Fonteyn – *some* prestidigitator does…. She *is* magic. She is Odette-Odile. She is Tchaikovsky. She, so absolutely British, is Russian Ballet. She, too, is a musician-magician, and the instrument she plays is her perfectly tuned, perfect-pitch-in-motion body. Don't talk to me of mere technique, or charisma, or of age, whatever that is. Just break, if you can, her spell."

Greer Johnson, on *Swan Lake*
Cue Magazine

Fonteyn is due to be seen again in America in October 1969, when she guests with the Washington National Ballet in a full-length version of the historic Romantic ballet *La Sylphide,* in which she flawlessly produces the required Bournonville 'manner'. She is partnered by Desmond Kelly (above) in the rôle of James The Highlander.

With Rudolf Nureyev and Keith Rosson, rehearsing Petit's ballet

Right, with Rudolf Nureyev as Pelléas

The première of the Petit ballet *Pelléas et Mélisande* at Covent Garden on 26th March had in fact marked Fonteyn's 35 years with the same company; *The Times* running a celebrated front page heading the following morning: "Queen Sees Fonteyn Take 10 Curtains", thus adding to the spate of people trying to avoid mentioning the ballet itself.

"Dame Margot Fonteyn is an international star on merit alone. The rather sickening apparatus of publicity, hired trains and junketings for the Press, guards' bands parading at ports, sheafs of adulatory handouts, may grind on for others but hardly for her.

Her audiences have never needed brain washing, pre-publicity, or over selling. She is simply the greatest dancer we have seen, and audiences everywhere respond to her quality. An American couple at the Gala Performance last Wednesday at Covent Garden to celebrate the 35 golden years she has graced our stage, appeared to know little of England and less about ballet. How they got there with seats almost unobtainable I cannot imagine. As the curtain fell, the woman turned to her husband and said "That girl's marvellous. Who is she?" He searched in the programme, and slowly spelt out "Margot Fonteyn."

Nicholas Dromgoole
Sunday Telegraph

"There are times when I could willingly strangle Margot Fonteyn, the hundredth anniversary of whose first appearance on the stage is now being celebrated throughout Europe and Central America.

She has been so well brought up either by her Mum or by that potent pedagogue Dame Ninette de Valois that she has perfected the art of answering questions at length and saying absolutely nothing. She would never, even under torture, admit that pink was her favourite colour for fear of offending orange and mauve.

This quality of old-school decency is allied to another of her outstanding characteristics – her loyalty. She is disgustingly loyal. She is not just loyal to her friends, and the Royal Ballet and the Queen: she is loyal to everyone. If she had a flop in a new ballet by an old friend you could be sure that he would be asked to do her *next* ballet for her. It is maddening."

Richard Buckle
Sunday Times

During the 14-week North American Tour, *Pelléas* continues doggedly in the repertoire, but it is performances in other ballets that claim attention:

"With something of the pomp and splendor due royalty, Dame Margot Fonteyn, accompanied of course by Rudolf Nureyev, made her return to New York Wednesday at the Metropolitan Opera House. She was dancing in the Royal Ballet's *Swan Lake*, and, fairly enough, endowed it with the special quality of grandeur that belongs to her very particular authority.

The great impresario Serge Diaghilev always declared that he was interested in ballerinas only when they were very young or very old. Dame Margot is far from being very old – but she does happen to be 50 in a few days' time, and might well be thought to have entered that interesting phase that separates the women from the girls.

What is unique about Dame Margot's portrayal of Odette/Odile is that through circumstances of ballet history she has danced more performances of this role – indeed all the great classic roles – than any other ballerina anywhere. Those same circumstances have virtually guaranteed that no-one else will ever match her record.

Dame Margot gave her first Odette/Odile in 1937, and in the last 32 years has given literally hundreds of performances. No other ballerina is likely to have the same opportunity. Hardly any dancer, except in a company's emergent years, is likely to get the role so young, or to dance it so often. And only very great dancers are able to maintain themselves into the 50's. But Fonteyn – here and now – looks good forever, or at least until she calls it quits. There have perhaps been physical losses over the years, but there have also been physical gains. Her line is as eloquent, as tearful as ever, her knees are still pulled up, her manner as musical, and for that matter, as untroubled. Wednesday night's Odette was exemplary. Dame Margot was technically impeccable, but also – if you accept the picture – technically guarded. But emotionally her dancing expressed precisely that curious Tchaikovsky lament of the Swan – that image of romanticism remote from reality, yet still real enough to die for. Fonteyn's Odette is all frozen pain and coldly crystallized understanding.

Mr. Nureyev is one of the finest Siegfrieds of our time – indeed, if we are counting, of any time. Yet when he dances with Fonteyn, he takes on a different cloak. Both know – having triumphed over so many laudatory press notices erecting their impossible standards of expectation – their true selves, and can dance them out with all the honesty of self-knowledge. Together they have the odd, essentially unbelievable magic of a legend made fact.

The Black Swan pas de deux, where the false and vicious Odile is poised unequally against the exuberant and trusting Siegfried, poses one of the greatest of all ballet equations. It is a test of technique, yes, but much more a test of style. For years there has been a foolish rumor that Dame Margot was more Odette than Odile – but this was never true, and has never been less true than now. Her adamantine brilliance as Odile – seen gloriously here – is never less brilliant for its touch of honest, occasionally even fallible, humanity. This is an Odile to betray an Odette for, and what more can one say?

In a sense the feeling of Dame Margot and Mr. Nureyev in the last act is almost the most impressive. Dame Margot is the final thread of a lost hope, while Mr. Nureyev, as assertive as a tiger, is the remembrance of an ultimate promise. Together they offer a world of feeling, a complex of emotions.

There are times when even the most devoted ballet fan wonders just what ballet can convey without the poetically vague, yet always imaginative specifics of words. And then you see a ballet by Balanchine or Ashton, a performance by Fonteyn and Nureyev, and you realize the challenging eloquence of silence."

Clive Barnes
The New York Times 1. 5. 69

SEQUENCE KEITH MONEY

In March 1970 Fonteyn guests with The Stuttgart Ballet, appearing with Richard Cragun in superb performances of *Swan Lake,* and starring in a new Cranko ballet mounted for her: *Poème de l'extase,* to Scriabin's music.

Courted by an ardent and impressionable young man, a beautiful diva in her Indian summer has thoughts only for distant, perfect loves. The young man is unable to compete with these virile images from the past.

The ballet's first performance on 24th March earns a rapturous reception.

Poème de l'extase

With Richard Cragun and Egon Madsen

With Madsen in the last moments of the ballet

Ashton Gala, New York 1970

The Royal Ballet's 12th visit to New York is celebrated as their 21st Anniversary season. For the programme honouring Ashton, and including his work, Fonteyn finds herself asked to dance in Petipa's *La Bayadère*. However she is seen on stage with Sir Frederick at the conclusion of the evening (above).

On 7th April she arrives in Finland for guest appearances in *The Sleeping Beauty*, with Attilio Labis, at the National Opera. From there she travels to Washington for the new production of *Cinderella,* staged by Ben Stevenson for the National Ballet.

On 24th July 1970, members of The Royal Ballet Company plan and rehearse (in secret) a remarkable retrospective Gala of Sir Frederick Ashton's work, as a tribute to their Director on his retirement from administrative duties. Among dozens of items, the audience sees Fonteyn in extracts from *Apparitions* and *Nocturne* (1936) and *The Wise Virgins* (1940), as well as *Daphnis and Chloë* (1951) and *Marguerite and Armand* (1963).

Ashton Galas

"But of all Ashton's dancers Margot Fonteyn has always been his jewel. Here miraculously – for unlike anyone else time has stopped for Dame Margot – she blithely danced some of the roles of her youth...

Then, almost unbelievably, as the lovers themselves (in *Daphnis and Chloë*) came Fonteyn and, yes, her old partner Michael Somes... and the audience cheered and cheered."

Clive Barnes
New York Times

Above,
The Wise Virgins,
1970

Top right,
Daphnis and Chloë
finale, 1970

Left,
Nocturne solo, 1970

Right,
Apparitions, 1970

Places and Partners 1970–1971

Right, Copenhagen,
Giselle with Flemming Flindt

Below, Milan,
The Sleeping Beauty with Rudolf Nureyev

Left, Dallas,
in George Skibine's Carmina Burana
with Attilio Labis

Right, Washington,
Cinderella with Desmond Kelly

Below right, Canberra,
Swan Lake with Garth Welch
(also Gayaneh)

Below, London,
La Bayadère with Keith Rosson
(later with David Wall)

Above, Gayaneh and, right, Swan Lake with Ivan Nagy,
during a tour with the Washington National Ballet

On 9th October 1970, on the 21st anniversary of her first appearance in America, Fonteyn appears in New York State in Ben Stevenson's production of *Cinderella* for Washington National Ballet.

"...But the youngest of all was Dame Margot, still the greatest ballerina in the world and also the most miraculous. Despite this, she is genuinely modest, a dancer who returns to the audience every jot of love she receives. She blooms like a rose before one's once more astonished eyes with the quiet authority of the indisputably unique. Again, hers was a triumph of dramatic and technical mastery expressed through a body almost mystically permeated with the phrasings and pulsations of the music."

Greer Johnson on *Cinderella*
Cue Magazine 24. 10. 70

With Robert Davis as Cinderella's father

The Sleeping Beauty

*Very much awake, with new productions
in Marseilles, Johannesburg and Washington*

"It is a gift as well as a defiance: she does not age, she gets younger... To play Princess Aurora since 1939 and to give the impression of not yet having completely absorbed it; to maintain intact the calculated perfection of an arabesque or a développé; to blossom on stage as a flower, not cut but with its roots well planted... to present the simplicity of the Sleeping Beauty with the velvety smile of a frightened faun; to be completely sure and yet completely naïve beside a partner who is at the height of his form and audacity – this is what the *prima ballerina assoluta* offered us at the Palais des Sports on Sunday evening."

Claude Sarraute
Le Monde

"Incredible Margot Fonteyn! At 52 years of age she remains the great *prima ballerina assoluta* of contemporary ballet. In a class of her own, with her technique and her intelligence. To dance the part of the Princess Aurora as she does at the Palais des Sports is partly prodigious, partly miraculous. Making pirouettes, balancing in a way that defies all the laws of elemental physics, she drops thirty years to become instantly the heroine of Tchaikovsky and Perrault as no-one else could.

Margot Fonteyn is not a declining star who still looks young, she is young with an inner fire that dazzles afresh each time she appears. Her Sleeping Beauty is a masterpiece of recreation. With her favourite partner Rudolf Nureyev, she displays a boundless femininity. She is simply marvellous. If only she could be eternal!"

Pierre Julien
L'Aurore

On 1st June 1971 she dances *Swan Lake* at Covent Garden with Nureyev.
"She was in magnificent form, dancing with her unique, enigmatic and exquisite finesse, making every movement seem created especially for her..."

Fernau Hall
Daily Telegraph

A week later she is doing the same thing in Munich in performances with Richard Cragun.

*Below, as light relief from performances of
The Sleeping Beauty in Johannesburg,
she finds herself the victim of a Students'
Rag Week 'kidnapping' ...*

With Nureyev in The Sleeping Beauty at the Palais des Sports in May

...with less skilled porterage

Rehearsing the
Aurora pas de deux
with Nureyev

*As the Nymph
of the Garden in*

Garden Party

As the Poet's Muse in

c. 1830

22nd June 1971. For an evening at the London Coliseum, organised by Richard Buckle to advertise, among other things, the need for English art lovers to contribute two million pounds if they wish to continue viewing Titian's painting "Death of Actaeon" on their own side of the Atlantic, Margot is at the centre of a notable assembly of guest artists. She appears in all three sections of the programme; first as The Nymph of the Garden in a ballet called *Garden Party*, choreographed by Peter Darrell to music by Bach; then in a *pas de deux* choreographed for the occasion by Ashton, as part of a ballet called *c. 1830*. In it, she dances with Desmond Kelly to the song *Oh, quand je dors* – one of several set to Liszt by Victor Hugo.

Finally, against Bakst's scenery and some of the costumes used by Diaghilev for his 1921 production of *The Sleeping Princess*, Fonteyn and Nureyev dance the great *pas de deux* from the last act. Michael Somes appears in the Minuet, and Anton Dolin and Alexandra Danilova appear as the King and the Queen.

As Aurora, with Rudolf Nureyev in **Aurora's Wedding**

In London, Margot rehearses *Raymonda* with Garth Welch, (above) before leaving for a tour of Australia in which she is to dance 26 performances of the three-act ballet. On the way South, she guests for a week with the Stuttgart Ballet in New York, appearing at the Met. in six performances of *Poème de l'extase*, before arriving in Perth, where she dances *Swan Lake* Act II and also the *Gayaneh pas de deux* – all with Welch. With The

Australian Ballet, she continues with more *Raymondas* during a visit to Manila and Singapore, interspersed with appearances in Milan (with Nureyev); with the Washington National Ballet in a new production by Ben Stevenson of *The Sleeping Beauty* (with Labis), and also in the Skibine version of *Romeo and Juliet* set to Berlioz' music (this too with Labis). In this extended *pas de deux* they make guest appearances in Miami.

On the possibility of a successor:

"You don't think about who will replace you when you aren't thinking of going."

Sydney Morning Herald
21. 10. 70

Raymonda in Australia

"Proud regality in her own right, and a rather wistful regality in characterisation, clothed Margot Fonteyn's name role performance in the Australian Ballet's production of *Raymonda*... Basic to this personal regality, and projecting it, is Fonteyn's superb control of technique. She is, like the truly great instrumental virtuoso or Test batsman, always in the right position at the right moment, always seeming to have time to spare.

As the lovely and initially lovelorn Raymonda, she moved without the slightest suggestion of muscular effort, and the pauses, utterly poised and motionless, were those hushed moments one marvels at in all the great virtuosi. And then, when she made her moves, she made them on her own terms; not on the demands of technique, or even, one suspected at times, of the choreographer. There was in her performance a great feeling of spontaneity. But surely, at this stage in her career, it must be a carefully polished 'effect' of spontaneity. Possibly it has a greater artistic quality.

I remember Gigli and Lotte Lehmann, long after their wonderful voices had lost their bloom, giving recitals and getting away with it by sheer artistry. But Fonteyn, at 52, hasn't reached this stage; by all the physical criteria she should have – but she hasn't. The bloom still suffuses the artistry."

Edward Lindall
The Australian 6. 8. 71

THE AGE

in Adelaide

Poème de l'extase in London

On 15th February 1972 *Poème de l'extase* opens, with The Royal Ballet, in London.

"... how beautiful Dame Margot looks, whether in the air or on the floor, she must be seen to be believed."
Annabel Farjeon
Evening Standard

Right, with David Drew, Desmond Kelly, David Wall, Peter O'Brien and Michael Coleman

SEQUENCE ROSEMARY WINCKE

with Michael Coleman

with Desmond Kelly

"Margot Fonteyn's performance in *Poème de l'extase*, which she danced for the first time in London last night, is a triumph on two levels. It is an extraordinary recreation of a whole style of art; that is what you notice first, but by the end of the ballet something else has emerged, and you realize that it is also a remarkable portrait of a woman... you have only to look at the curves and tendrils of Fonteyn's body and arms at any moment of the ballet to see the whole Jugendstil burst into vivid life. It is an astonishing act of artistic identification."

John Percival
The Times 16. 2. 72

J.B. PRIESTLEY ON THE GOLDEN DAYS OF QUEEN VICTORIA

With evocative paintings, reprinted in full colour, by fashionable artists of the day.

Poster protest for Dame Margot

by ROSALIND MORRIS

A SMALL group of protesters led by anti-apartheid campaigner Peter Hain and his parents confronted Dame Margot Fonteyn yesterday as she left the Royal Opera House, Covent Garden, after a matinee performance.

Some of the protesters carried posters: 'Don't dance to the apartheid tune.'

Dame Margot is to give a series of performances in Cape Town later this month before segregated audiences.

The Coloured Labour Party in South Africa has called for a mass demonstration at Cape Town airport when she arrives on 26 April, to be followed by protests outside her hotel and at two Cape Town theatres where she will dance in 'Swan Lake.'

At Covent Garden, Dame Margot, who had been dancing in 'Poème de l'Extase,' spoke briefly to Mr Hain, who handed her a letter before she was driven away by her chauffeur at rapid speed.

She was in good humour—unlike some of her fans who had also been waiting for her outside Covent Garden. They tore up some of the protesters' posters.

Mr Hain said he believed the demonstration had been a success because he had been able to talk to Dame Margot. 'She said she [...] t she did [...]

Dame Margot argues with critics of apartheid

From Michael Knipe
Cape Town, April 19

Dame Margot Fonteyn arrived in Cape Town today for a controversial series of performances before segregated audiences and in a confrontation with airport demonstrators expressed her categoric disapproval of apartheid.

"I'm very happy to see you here," she said, smiling radiantly, as she was surrounded by young whites and non-whites displaying placards with such slogans as "Don't dance to the apartheid tune," "Shame on you" and "Boycott in the name of human dignity and self respect."

She stood back and read out aloud the slogan on one banner: "No true Christian accepts apartheid." "I agree," she said. "Who says I accept apartheid?"

Several hundred people took part [...]

people?" Dame Margot replied: "Yes, but doesn't it make more point if I come here and you can demonstrate like this?"

At a press conference she was asked for her reaction to the demonstration. "I thought those people were very right," she said. "The posters they held up were quite justified. I am sympathetic to them."

She had heard that there was going to be a boycott of her performances but not that bookings for her performances for non-whites were very slack.

She had come to dance and it did not concern her whether she danced before two people or two thousand. "I think people who don't want to go to that theatre because they feel it's an indignity are absolutely right", Dame Margot added. "I personally can't understand why they can't see the performance in the opera house. It doesn't make sense to me. I quite understand how they feel. I'm sure I'd feel the same".

For a [...] 1955, sh [...] tions to [...] " and th [...] The fact [...] munist c [...] she supp [...] did her [...] Africa [...] aparthei [...]

She d [...] coming [...] could s [...] was imp [...] stand or [...] but as a [...] she had [...] refuse to [...]

The [...] and the [...] African [...] boycott [...] formanc [...] whites.

DAVID NEWELL SMITH

[...] lain, with anti- [...] l poster, talking Margot Fonteyn he Royal Opera House.

[...] audiences and these are being held at another theatre.

Opponents of apartheid believe that performers of Dame Margot's stature are giving valuable assistance to the system by agreeing to appear before whites-only audiences at the Nico Malan.

Dame Margot displayed both self-assurance and sympathy as she walked among the demonstrators today. They were equally polite.

"Do you realize they rely on your support?" asked one white youth.

"Personally, I don't agree with you", Dame Margot said. "No one would know if I had refused to come here."

A coloured young man said: "Don't you understand the insult your performance will be to black

---

Why Dame Margot won't be bullied

I APPLAUD Fonteyn's refusal to be bullied into cancelling her engagements in South Africa. Dame Margot combined a protest—by insisting on dancing for black as well as white audiences—with help to a fellow artist, the director of the Cape Town Ballet. To ask more is inviting her to forsake her art for the dubious business of instructing politicians and other countries a la marching Miss Redgrave who had the temerity to poke her nose into an Irish issue that defeated even the mighty Shaw!

Instead of forcing the world's only prima ballerina assoluta to make statements to the Press, her fans should be agitating that she—and the splendid de Valois who founded the company that fostered and brought Fonteyn's art to fruition—be accorded the equivalent of Olivier's honour, a peerage.

Admittedly, a Dame is a Dame is a Dame, as Gertrude Stein might have said but [...]

Whites 'black up' to see Fonteyn dance

By DAVID LOSHAK in Cape Town

WHITE women wore saris and brown pancake make-up and men wore dark glasses to get into a performance for coloured people only in Cape Town —their last chance to see Dame Margot Fonteyn dance in South Africa.

Dame Margot was appearing in Swan Lake, and due to a boycott against segregated performances, hundreds of Coloured people stayed away.

The Whites, who attended risked prosecution. Outside the hall, well away from Cape Town Opera House, where Dame Margot gave her main perform-

ances for all-White audiences, a small group demonstrated against the necessity for separate performances for different races.

It was an ironic end to Dame Margot's South African visit that she should have danced before a mixed audience, in view of the Government's persistent refusal to change its ruling on strict segregation.

Before leaving Cape Town, Dame Margot said she would not encourage other overseas artists to visit South Africa. It was a decision for each individual. She was pleased with her own visit and felt she had done the right thing by coming.

Fear for Lor[...]

Margot tells why she said 'yes' and 'no'

By SYDNEY EDWARDS

DAME MARGOT FONTEYN explained in London today why she accepted an invitation to dance in South Africa and the reasons why she will not give in to pressure to make her cancel her visit.

In New York today the United Nations Special Committee made public a letter it had written to Dame Margot asking her not to appear in South Africa.

"I'd already accepted to go by the time I got the letter from The U.N. Committee on Apartheid," said Dame Margot. "If I refused after that then that would be a political action and I'm not getting involved in political action.

Right thing

" How many dozen times have I refused in the past to dance in South Africa? I did not go there at all between 1955 and 1971. I'm going this time for purely ballet reasons. David Poole, an old friend from the Royal Ballet, now runs the Cape Town Ballet and it seemed there would be some advantage to his company if I came to dance in their new Swan Lake.

"I'm convinced the right thing to do is to go, in all the circumstances. I will also be dancing for coloured people. One makes sure of that.

"If you live outside South Africa then you cannot possibly have any sympathy for apartheid. It is awful and it doesn't make any sense.

"In Panana (where Dame Margot lived with her husband) it doesn't exist.

"I don't mind if there will be protests. That can't be helped. I'll stick to my course and my business. I'm an artist and artists should not make demonstrations. You should concentrate and get on with what you have to do and do it the best you can.

"If I'm going to protest about something I should do it in England because I' mEnglish. I'm entitled to do it here. I did not mind the demonstration outside the stage door at Covent Garden last weekend. They did it very well. But I don't think you go to other countries and tell them their business.

"I won't be pushed into making this action. If they want to demonstrate against me that's fair enough. It's my bad luck.

"I think it would be cowardly and wrong of me to cancel after I'd accepted just to retain the admiration of my fans who had not thought it all out. I'd be rather ashamed if I did that.

"I think the people who want to make protests are trying to use me and I don't feel it is my place to make the actual protest. You either accept or not. I accepted for ballet reasons.

"The real point is that if I had turned them down in the first place who would have known? There would have been no headlines. And what difference would it have made to the South African government? An empty gesture."

DAME MARGOT FONTEYN

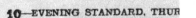

OVERSEAS NEWS

Dame Margot protest

CAPETOWN, Thursday.—A crowd of anti-apartheid demonstrators carrying placards greeted Dame Margot Fonteyn when she arrived here for performances of Swan Lake—but the prima ballerina said later that she sympathised with them.

Dame Margot is to dance for whites-only in the Nico Malan on Saturday, but will perform for a non-white audience in a week's time.

After the demonstration she told a Press conference: " I think these people are very right and I support them and I personally can't understand why everyone shouldn't see the production in the Nico Malan Opera House." (Reuter).

Sadat for Moscow

FONTEYN BOYCOTT

Whites-only dance

OUR STAFF CORRESPONDENT in Cape Town cabled: Dr Marius Barnard, brother of Prof. Christiaan Barnard, said yesterday that he supported the proposed boycott of the Cape Town theatre where Dame Margot Fonteyn is due to dance before an all-White audience next month.

Dame Margot agreed to stage an additional performance for Coloured people at a suburban theatre.

THE TIMES FRIDAY APRIL 21 1972

collects ~~£290,000~~ them, and in 1970-71 its investments, valued at around £1,052,000 b r o u g h t in £38,574.

A RESCUE operation for Dame Margot Fonteyn: setting off for South Africa on the visit which has aroused some anti-apartheid controversy, she was faced with the problem of getting to the airport on time, through the traffic jams. Mr Charles Hughesden, the company director and husband of Florence Desmond, lent her his helicopter to fly her from Battersea to Heathrow. "I don't think she would have got there otherwise," he tells me.

Covent Garden ~~whispers~~

~~...ago I reported~~

Dame Margot Fonteyn, arriving in Cape Town to fulfil ballet engagements before segregated audiences, keeps smiling despite the protests.

the over-all shape of the performance, the supreme art that gives the rôle its glow of life and truth, was superbly in evidence. My programme for the evening bears hastily scribbled remarks about her artistry in the Rose Adagio, about her delicacy of phrasing in the vision scene, and about the stylistic rightness of her line for Petipa; but ultimately I must record that Fonteyn dances Aurora by divine right, and still enhances the rôle... the evening – and the ballet – belonged as it always has, to Fonteyn."

Clement Crisp
Financial Times 7. 4. 72

On 24th February 1972, for the Sadler's Wells Appeal Fund, Margot appears in a Midnight Gala, as The Girl in *Le Spectre de la Rose,* partnered for the first time by Anthony Dowell. It is a nostalgic Fonteyn appearance. But for the war, her début in the same ballet twenty-nine years previously would have taken place on the same stage – rather than the New Theatre where the company had been transferred.

At Easter, she appears with David Wall in a Benefit Performance in Miami, dancing the *Aurora pas de deux.*

In Raymonda Act III, with Anthony Dowell as Jean de Brienne

London

"If there is any single image which evokes The Royal Ballet it is that of Dame Margot Fonteyn in *The Sleeping Beauty.* It is a key image, a crucial one in its implication of classic excellence, and one which I must be pardoned for saying dates back to 1939. And last night it was still blazingly true, and still marvellous.

Great art in the theatre must ultimately defy description: in ballet we can talk of line, musicality, of classic grace, harmony and authority, in speaking of Fonteyn, and the essence of her greatness will escape us. I could, indeed, state quite succinctly that last night Fonteyn's Aurora was profoundly moving, and then leave well alone, since no words can adequately convey just why her performance was so heartening. Critical duty – and a desire, I suppose, to express my own sense of gratitude – impels me to note that Dame Margot brought a total conviction to the rôle, that her dancing was marvellously proportioned (no extravagance, but a simplicity that bespeaks complete understanding of the choreography) and a musicality in phrasing that makes the dance a perfect extension of the score.

A few of her effects were more restrained than heretofore, but

New York

The 13th New York season by The Royal Ballet begins in the Spring.

"Dame Margot Fonteyn has not been seen in New York in *Swan Lake* for two years. On Wednesday night with the Royal Ballet at the Metropolitan Opera House her Odette/Odile returned to us, luminous and passionate. Dame Margot has danced Odette/Odile longer and more often than any other ballerina has ever danced or probably ever will.

She danced her first Odette in 1935 at the age of 16 and she danced the complete ballet three years later. I have been watching her dance Odette/Odile for 30 years and writing about it for more than 20. I mention all this because I want to stress, not for the present but for the future record, the unique aspect of Dame Margot's achievement.

Many classic ballerinas outstay their welcome by a few years, and it is a critical custom – not upheld, I think, by myself, to lie a little about their prowess. A dancer's career is often so short, and the tragedy of its decline is sometimes thought to be worth a few white lies on the way down for dues paid and services rendered. I hasten to assure posterity that Dame Margot needs none of this. She is not just the best 53-year-old ballerina in the business, she is still, without qualification, the greatest ballerina in the world. Shakespeare was wrong – age does wither but with Dame Margot it has burnished.

There have been some losses. Obviously, physically it is not easy to do the impossible. She should have suffered considerable diminution of technique by this time, and frankly she has suffered very little. I notice that she now settles in the Black Swan *pas de deux* for 24 decent *fouettes* rather than the 32 stipulated by tradition but which even in her youth – indeed particularly in her youth – she frequently flubbed. Her balances are fantastic, her line remains as eloquent as ever, and her dancing shows pressure but little strain.

Odette/Odile has been one of her great roles, not perhaps so identified with her as Aurora in *The Sleeping Beauty,* but perhaps more challenging. Over the years and decades, she has made this into a wonderfully complete portrayal. The dual sexuality and the poetic myth, the romantic image of love in death, all these she locates in the story. Her dancing comes from the music – she acts in symbols but moves with Tchaikovsky. It is a lovely performance and, in its detail of personification, seemingly complete. Maturity is terribly rare in dance, and Fonteyn has achieved it. She is that luckiest of dancers who has always managed to make her present into her prime."

Clive Barnes
New York Times 6. 5. 72

4th June; on the last night of The Royal Ballet's New York season, Fonteyn, as Aurora, produces yet again one of her most breathtaking Rose Adagios. In an uncanny flashback to the famous night in 1949 the audience is mesmerised by the perfection of each step, the utter inevitability of the balances. Once more, the proferred hands of the supporting princes appear to be entirely superfluous. Aurora remains isolated, crowned by right and youthfully supreme. In the wings, her fellow dancers are unable to resist joining in the screams of the audience; one of them says "Well, *that's* why we come to New York!" And New York responds, as only New York can. The audience has already stood *en masse* and sung "Happy Birthday" during curtain calls on the eve of Margot's 53rd birthday.

From an exhaustive tour of America leading the Vienna State Opera Ballet, with which she has danced innumerable *Swan Lakes,* partnered by Karl Musil, Fonteyn arrives back in London, in time to pay tribute to a fellow Dame.

On 29th October 1972 an extraordinary galaxy of the great names in British Theatre assembles in a programme to do honour to Dame Sybil Thorndike on the occasion of her 90th birthday.

"Artistically, perhaps the high point of the night was Margot Fonteyn's dance, with David Wall, from *The Sleeping Beauty.* The perennially youthful ballerina brought this off with such a fling of delight that it left the air signed with her grace."

John Barber
The Daily Telegraph 30. 10. 72

There follow two performances of *Raymonda* Act III at Covent Garden, with Margot partnered by Anthony Dowell.

"It was certainly an object lesson in star quality to see Fonteyn transform a routine performance by the company into a very special and memorable occasion.

'At least you can say you have seen Fonteyn,' what looked like an aunt said to what looked like a small nephew after the performance. She said it in a tone of voice which implied he might never have much else to offer, but he suddenly asserted himself. 'Yes,' he said, 'and I want to see her again as soon as possible.'

So do I."

Nicholas Dromgoole
The Sunday Telegraph 12. 11 72

ALAN CUNLIFFE

291

Above,
with David Wall in
Birthday Offering,
in London

Opposite page,
with Heinz Bosl,
rehearsing The
Sleeping Beauty
in Berlin . . .

. . . and with
Karl Musil,
taking a curtain
call after George
Skibine's love
scene from Romeo
and Juliet,
in Reykjavik

Left and below,
with Attilio Labis
in the same ballet,
in Washington

But the wear and tear of the schedule brings on some physical damage, and a sudden return to the choreographic intricacies (disguised for so long) in *Birthday Offering* is judged by some to be a mistake, though John Percival writes:

"On the other hand, I must say I enjoyed *Birthday Offering* more than some of my colleagues. True, Fonteyn cannot bring to her solo, with all those little tripping steps, the glitter she showed in 1956, but the way she crosses the stage at the beginning of the pas de deux still sends a shudder down my spine, and in fact she presents this opulent duet with a more confident flourish now than when she first danced it."

From London Margot travels to Leeds (where she had arrived in 1939 to find war declared and ballet performances cancelled) this time to appear in the Skibine version of *Romeo and Juliet*, in which she is partnered by Attilio Labis. The evening goes well, but two nights later, in London, *Swan Lake* finds flutterings of anxiety from beyond the footlights: the critics concerned than an *assoluta* should be seen to be absolute.

On 4th December *The Guardian* publishes a leading article by James Kennedy, with a heading made of the quote "I cannot endure it that a new image of diminished, studiously economical dancing should oust the memories of unanxious greatness."

In the long retrospective article on Fonteyn he suggests that critics have begun to surround Margot with a conspiracy of affection, saying nothing unkind about "this beloved dancer, who, at 53, remains the Queen of British ballet."

No conspiracy seemed particularly evident in the critiques of the week preceding the article's publication; candour being notably apparent:

"The presence of Dame Margot Fonteyn in *Swan Lake* has been for many of us one of the most thrilling images of our national ballet. Her account of Odette-Odile has been an exemplar for apprentice ballerinas, a yardstick for measuring foreign artists; returning to the lake last night she demonstrated in the first *pas de deux* a grandeur of imagery that came from a noble simplicity and a total directness of statement, so that music and dance seemed one.

This was a shining pinnacle in an evening that otherwise found Dame Margot below form; her control and understanding of the whole drama are still magnificent, but though her interpretation had beauties of phrasing and a rare eloquence of expression – notably in Act IV – there was also a technical constraint that dulled the impact of much of the ballet. This is not a matter of the substitution of *piqué* turns for the Act III *fouettes,* which is a vulgar trick anyway, but rather a question of a loss of clarity and a feeling of physical forces too carefully husbanded. If it seems ungracious to carp at a muted Fonteyn performance, since the artistry is still unrivalled in its ability to show the very heart of this most popular of ballets, let me add that my standards are of the highest because established by Dame Margot herself."

Clement Crisp
The Financial Times

"And on Monday the old Fonteyn magic – which had looked rather dimmed at the recent Gala – flashed out again in an eloquent rendering of *Swan Lake* with David Wall."

Alexander Bland
The Observer

At Leeds:

"Then came Margot Fonteyn and Attilio Labis in George Skibine's *Romeo and Juliet pas de deux* to music by Berlioz. Descending shyly from her balcony, the divine creature was caressed, cradled, laid on the floor, held at arm's length and borne aloft by her agile partner. She timed her little spinning diagonals and extended in arabesque as prettily as ever. We basked in her glamour. Labis got in some fine leaps and spins, but for the most part he hardly let go of Fonteyn. It was a work calculated to show off the great dancer's artistry without over-taxing her physical power.

This could not be said of *Swan Lake* which I had seen her perform at Covent Garden on Monday. There was still magic in Act II but, adoring her as I do, I should not wish her to embark on the ordeal of Act III ever again."

Richard Buckle
The Sunday Times

A few days later she is in Nottingham, standing in for an injured colleague – in three performances of – inevitably – the "Black Swan" *pas de deux*.

On 26th December 1972 she makes an appeal on television for relief aid for victims of the earthquake in Nicaragua – where she had appeared earlier in the year.

Back at Covent Garden, she is joined by Nureyev in the current production of *Swan Lake* with the Petipa Act IV restored.

"In *Swan Lake* last night Dame Margot Fonteyn demonstrated for all the world to see that she is Odette still. And Odile, too. An earlier performance this season had found her far below her usual illustrious form, and lovers of her interpretation might be excused for fearing that the glory had departed. But not so, if this present reading is anything to go by. With Nureyev as her Siegfried, Dame Margot once again established that control of the ballet that is the perogative of a great artist. Her interpretation may now be more careful in its husbanding of physical effects, but Fonteyn's was never a virtuoso display; the grandeur was of phrasing, musicality and poetic intensity, and so it marvellously remains. It is a performance of a supreme dance intelligence, which understands and can express the most crucial matters of the ballet.

The result in the lake-side scenes is a characterisation that convinces us utterly by its lyricism; and, as if to disprove the prophets of change and decay, the ball-room duet had a physical force and a mimetic brilliance that are to be preferred to more obviously glittering statements from ballerinas who mistake virtuosity for art."

Clement Crisp
Financial Times 12. 1. 73

"As the Swan Queen, Fonteyn is unmatched for the way she phrases her dancing to the melancholy of Tchaikovsky's music. She herself has danced the steps with more clarity in the past, but she can still make more of them than some of her younger rivals in the role. Above all, she brings to the elegiac last act a sense of resigned sorrow that is deeply touching."

John Percival
The Times 12. 1. 73

13th January 1973; for a special Gala Performance at the Royal Opera House, Covent Garden, Fonteyn joins leading dancers from six other European companies to celebrate the entry of Great Britain into the European Economic Community. A new year, and a new era, begins. For Fonteyn, another aeroplane and another stage await.

A Career in Curtain Calls

*After her first performance in
The Sleeping Princess, 1939*

*After Daphnis and Chloë
on the eve of her marriage,
1955*

After Swan Lake – the night after being awarded a D.B.E., 1956

After The Sleeping Beauty; last night in Melbourne, 1957

Left, after Giselle; the first Covent Garden performance following release from jail in Panama, 1959

Below, after the Sylvia pas de deux in Monte Carlo, 1956; with Somes and Anton Dolin – with whom Fonteyn danced the Aurora pas de deux at the Nijinsky Gala in 1937

After Swan Lake; in Tokyo, 1959

After Ondine; opening night at the Bolshoi, 1961

In costume from Spectre, after presenting Rudolf Nureyev to English audiences for the first time, at the R.A.D. Charity Gala, 1961

After Beauty and the Beast, in New Zealand, 1962

After the first performance of Marguerite and Armand, 1963

*Left, after
the New York
opening of
Marguerite
and Armand*

*Right,
after
Le Corsaire's
first
New York
performance,
1963*

After Swan Lake; awarded the City of Paris' special prize, First International Dance Festival, 1963

Right, after Les Sylphides,
with Nureyev, in America

After Le Corsaire; the presentation of tourmaline and diamond earrings on the occasion of her 20th anniversary in New York, 1969

SEQUENCE V. SLADON

With Senator Jacob Javits, impresario Sol Hurok and Rudolf Nureyev

*With Nureyev, after the fourth performance of
The Sleeping Beauty in three days at Marseilles,
1971*

With Karl Musil, after Swan Lake, 1972

MILTON GREENE

306

Coming out of an elevator in New York one day, she remarks:
　"Oh! It's raining."
The elevator attendant is heard to reply:
　"Yes, ma'am, but *you* can walk between the raindrops."

"I only think of what I must do tomorrow – that I must dance *Swan Lake*, that I must dance *Sleeping Beauty*. I go from day to day. I don't clutter up my mind with a lot of externals and things I have no control over. Perhaps I *survive* by not thinking about all these things. All I'm concerned about is concentrating more and more on what has to be done, and I feel I must work continually harder.... I suspect I'll go on dancing until I can't any more. But, I assure you, I don't think about it. I only think about doing things well."

in an interview by John Gruen
The New York Times 28. 5. 72

March 28, 1970
Stuttgart, Germany

Dearest Miss Fonteyn,

If the way you do
everything could be
summed up into one word,
that word would be the
most beautiful word in
the world.

Thank You,
With All My
Admiration,
Mark H. Neal

The Haunted Ballroom

Les Sylphides
*Uncle Remus

Rio Grande
*The Lord of Burleigh

Les Rendezvous

Swan Lake

Apparitions

Aida

Nocturne

Pomona
*Checkmate

Horoscope

The Judgement of Paris

The Sleeping Beauty

A pictorial index of ballets in which Margot Fonteyn has danced a leading rôle, 1935–1973

*denotes picture not availab.

Carnaval
(First as Papillon, later as Columbine)

Façade

Lysistrata

Baiser de la Fée

Casse-Noisette

Giselle
*Prometheus

Les Patineurs

A Wedding Bouquet

Dante Sonata
*Cupid and Psyche

The Wise Virgins

The Wanderer

Orpheus and Eurydice

Comus

Hamlet

The Rake's Progress

Coppélia

The Fairy Queen

Le Tricorne

Mam'zelle Angot

Scènes de Ballet

Ballet Imperial

Le des Sirènes

Daphnis and Chloë

Tiresias

314

The Quest

Le Spectre de la Rose
*Promenade

Symphonic Variations

Les Sirènes

Les Demoiselles de la Nuit

Don Juan

Cinderella

Don Quixote

Sylvia

Homage to The Queen

L'Entrée Japonaise

The Firebird

La Péri

Birthday Offering

Petrushka

Ondine

Marguerite and Armand

La Sylphide

La Bayadère

Divertimento

The Fairie Queene

Paradise Lost

Night Shadow

Pelléas et Mélisande

Scène d'Amour

Beauty and the Beast

Le Corsaire

Gayaneh

Raymonda

Paquita

The Dying Swan

Romeo and Juliet

Poème de l'extase

Carmina Burana

Garden Party

c1830

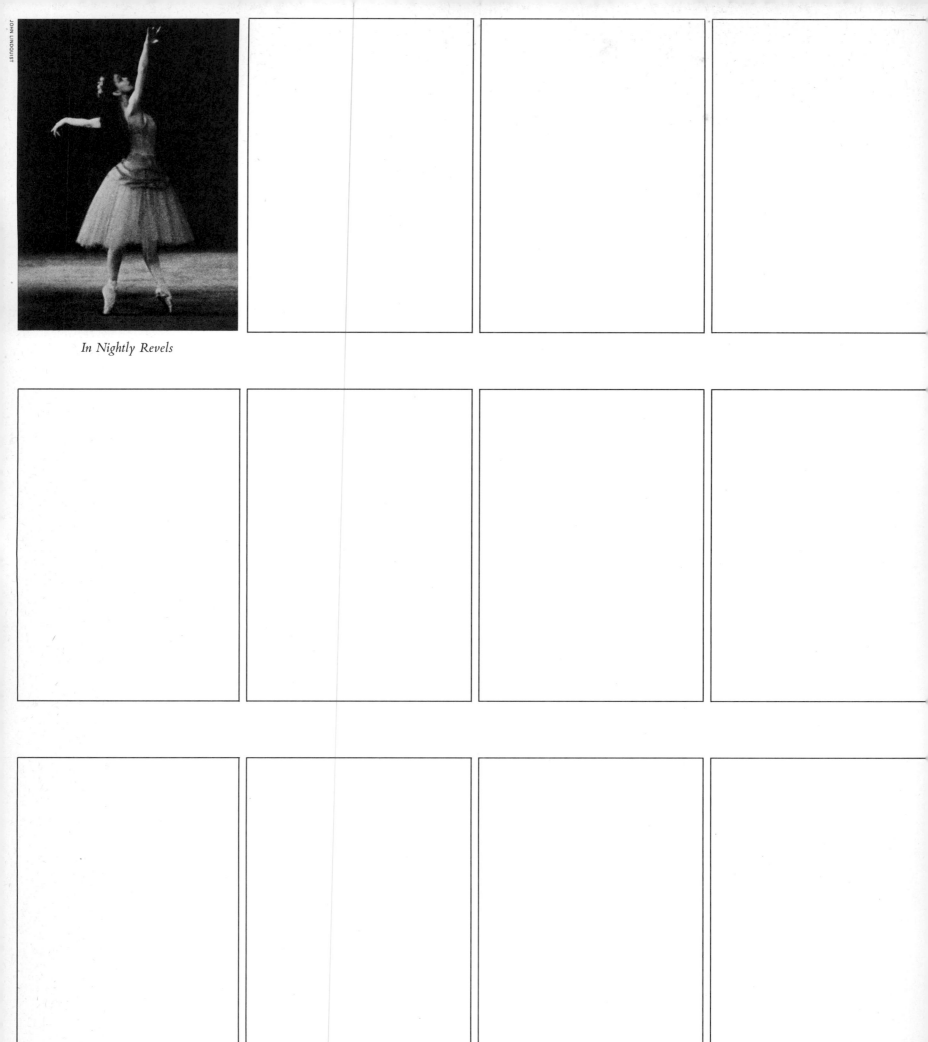

In Nightly Revels

Index

Italic figures indicate illustrations